MW01113825

The Hybrid Business School:
Developing Knowledge Management through Management Learning

Walter Baets
Gert van der Linden

The Hybrid Business School:
Developing Knowledge Management
through Management Learning

An imprint of Pearson Education

Amsterdam • Auckland • Bangkok • Bogota • Bonn • Buenos Aires
Cape Town • Don Mills • Harlow • Hong Kong • Jakarta • Madrid
Manila • Melbourne • Mexico • Milan • Puerto Rico • Reading
Santiago • Selangor • Seoul • Singapore • Sydney • Taipei • Tokyo

ISBN 90-430-0223-2
NUGI: 684

Coverdesign: Helma Timmermans, Amsterdam
Editing: Re*actie* Utrecht
Typeset: BEELDVORM, Leidschendam
Printing: A-D Druk, Zeist

To Jana, Carmen and Derk-Jan

About the authors

Walter Baets holds the Philips Chair in Information and Communication Technology at Nyenrode University, the Netherlands Business School, and is director of the Nyenrode Ph.D. Program. He is director of Notion, the Nyenrode Institute for Knowledge Management and Virtual Education, a competence center sponsored by Achmea, Microsoft, Philips and Sara Lee/DE. He graduated in Econometrics and Operations Research at the University of Antwerp (Belgium) and took a postgraduate degree in Business Administration at the Warwick Business School (UK). He was awarded a Ph.D. in Industrial and Business Studies by the University of Warwick. After pursuing a career of more than ten years in business, he held academic positions in Belgium, Russia, the Netherlands and Spain. He was particularly active in management development both in Russia and the Arab world.

A selection of the titles that Walter Baets wrote and (co-)edited are the following: *IT and Organizational Transformation*, Baets, W. & B. Galliers (1998), Wiley; *Organizational Learning and Knowledge Technologies in a Dynamic Environment*, Baets, W. (1998), Kluwer Academic Publishers; *A Collection of Essays on Complexity and Management*, Baets, W. ed. (1999), World Scientific.

Gert van der Linden is affiliated to several business schools and business institutes in France, Spain, Belgium, and Sweden. He has been involved in conceptualizing, designing, and coordinating several innovative management development programs and strategies as well as Corporate MBA and Leadership/ Top Executive Programs for several major European, Japanese, and American companies. He graduated in Organizational Psychology, and took a postgraduate degree in Management and Technology at the Free University of Brussels. He holds a Ph.D. in Business Administration from the University of Groningen.

A founding member of the GP Group, Gert van der Linden has acted as advisor and consultant for several international companies and senior managers. He is active in facilitating defining, developing and implementing strategic processes and management development strategies. He acted as an interim/transition manager for several international companies. Most of his ten years of professional experience was acquired in the technology sector.

Contents

Foreword

It is a pleasure to write the introduction to this book.

While reading this book, I appreciated the way the authors described clearly a consistent picture of knowledge and learning. I was pleasantly surprised to realize that I recognized many of the challenges and topics discussed from my own managerial practice, not only as an individual, but also as the president of a multinational corporation. I was able to see that a number of the knowledge theoretical and philosophical questions discussed in the book deal in a structured way with questions that I myself often face in day to day management. The authors are able to describe an environment that allows learning and sharing of experiences within larger corporations in a creative yet logical way. Most importantly, however, is that their original advice given on how to create a process of continuous self-development of managers, within a new framework and philosophy designed for the modern age of fast-moving companies and time scarcity, can actually be practically realized and is not just an intangible idealistic idea. Life-long learning becomes therefor a reality.

An important responsibility I have is to identify how to continuously find value in and use the potential of our huge human capital. I am constantly searching also for innovative ways to help people learn from each other's experiences, independent of time and space.

This book presents a readable explanation to managers and academics of the important potential of knowledge management and virtual education. It offers a chance to satisfy intellectual curiosity and the need for practical guidelines in this field. This book provides a practical guide that does not only address existing questions, but equally gives clear guidelines for successful implementation of learning from one another's experiences, and this as much locally as globally. As I have personally benefited from the practical material pertaining to knowledge management and virtual education, I am quick to recommend it to all those who want to take their personal development in their own hands and find the ammunition to sell the concept and ideas within their own organization.

Cor Boonstra
President of Philips
Amsterdam, januari 2000

Love and development are the two most precious gifts a person can give.

In the first context, we are indebted to our loved ones who nurture, cultivate, and enrich us.

In the second context, we think the greatest gift that can be offered to young management talent is development through state-of-the-art organizational insights and management knowledge. New pressures on managers due to the increased complexity in the new economy reiterate the need and relevance for continuous development. During our own careers as students and scholars, however, we have experienced not only how difficult it is to enable people to develop effectively, but also how management should be approached (or not). We therefore dedicate this book to all those involved in people's development, and hope we can be of help in offering that gift.

Our sincere gratitude goes to Pamela Parker for her unfailing patience and devotion in editing this book.

Introduction

Today most Business Schools are experimenting with distance learning and online education. Similarly many companies are creating their own corporate universities or learning centers, as companies become more knowledgeable about and interested in competency based management education that derives from corporate knowledge, which are often virtual. This combination of learning and knowledge management can lead to a new form of on-line learning that caters for practising managers in a just-in-time, just-enough way. Companies want to learn from their own experience and to be able to further enhance that experience with best principles and lessons learned from other companies. This book is intended to address that need.

Companies want to combine management education with knowledge management in a way that reinforces both. Clearly managers will often have some idea of the complexities of managing this process, and business schools should be able to incorporate their ideas into their programs. Doing so, however, requires that managers and business schools share a common understanding of the philosophy and purpose of education and of knowledge management. We are still a long way from that common understanding: this book attempts to bring these two worlds together.

This book addresses the interests both companies and business schools have in being able to combine life-long learning with knowledge management. Certainly we advocate this approach, but we go further too: we explain the value behind it, discuss the theories developed around it, and give clear guidelines for development, both for companies and business schools alike.

Naturally companies want to learn from their experience and they learn to share these lessons with employees. Briefly, best practices are interesting stories; best principles are lessons learned that can be applied in new projects. Employees should be empowered to learn from past failures and benefit from best practices as these are translated into best principles. The reader, and managers in particular, will find this book a useful guide into setting up a platform for knowledge sharing and/or common learning. Our approach is to apply principles deriving from educational theory to the needs of companies for just-in-time, just-enough learning.

We discuss innovative ideas in the field of education and give practical guidelines that companies and educational institutes wanting to learn from the experience of web-based teaching. Learning from experience is of course crucial, offer material for reflection and self-learning we find useful. Our approach is to guide the reader throughout a concrete plan of steps 'to do'.

If you join us on our exploratory tour of these exiting forms of management development, you can expect to reap an understanding of the following issues.

In chapter 1, we explain our interpretation of the present economic environment, such as the new economic realities, and the agents of change that companies encounter these days. The telecom (r)evolution and, more generally, technological evolution, will receive particular attention, since they are often the cause of discontinuities in corporate development, and the appropriate use of IT remains an important concern of corporations today. It is the general collapse of time and space that has led to the creation of the knowledge era that is ours, which has particularities of its own.

We relate the knowledge era to the dynamic behaviour of systems. The understanding of some of the fundamental concepts discussed, allows the reader to consider knowledge and learning from a completely different angle, and view them as the paradigms of learning by doing.

Chapter 2 describes the impact of the knowledge economy on the corporate environment, where changing managerial roles and the necessary managerial competencies are identified, and where we witness a movement from classical control-based management to a more networked organization. As managers have more hybrid roles and operate on different levels in different functions, and as they become involved in the play itself rather than just be the director, we will pinpoint the competencies needed in order for them to adequately fulfill this new hybrid role.

Another important development in the corporate environment is the role that information is increasingly playing, and more particularly, the dynamic process by which information is continually created and adapted. This dynamic property of information contrasts strongly with the static character of the Information Systems (IS) development, which tends to be fatally out of date by the time it becomes available. A promising area is therefore that of adaptive and learning applications – applications that 'learn' and change by doing. Some attention is given to artificial neural networks as a practical example of a learning software development tool.

The relationships between knowledge and experience, learning and mental models, and knowledge and learning are discussed in order to clarify why knowledge management should be made available via a learning platform. Also, the complex process of learning and the concept of organizational learning is explained in the context of the (post)modern company. It is intentional that this book does not focus on concepts but simply uses them to support our framework. In addition, it offers practical guidelines to those who would like to incorporate our ideas and programs into their own companies and business institutes.

Chapter 3 focusses on to the business education environment. In it, some of the criticism of business on business schools and business education are investigated. An inventory of practical experiences of management development in its broadest sense is made, and the chapter will deal with phenomena such as long-distance learning, corporate universities and corporate MBAs. Eventually, this will lead to the development of an educational competency approach, with details on program design and teaching philosophy.

Building a virtual corporate learning platform naturally cannot be done without some state of the art information technology. Chapter 4 shows the influence of knowledge management on virtual education, based on information and knowledge technologies such as case-based reasoning systems, group decision support systems, artificial neural networks, and knowledge platforms. Information about learning environments and on the latest developments in communication technology will present a clear picture of how knowledge management and virtual education can be combined: this is what we call the Hybrid Business School.

Chapter 5 presents a detailed discussion of the concept of the Hybrid Business School by paying attention to the necessary building blocks, but equally focusing on the methodology and process of implementation. This chapter emphasizes what is happening today in on-line lifelong learning, focussing on the concerns of companies and actual managers. Virtual learning fuses with knowledge management, thus creating a 'learning' and adaptable knowledge platform for companies. By the end of this chapter, the reader will be able to design his own virtual learning method in support of knowledge management.

Next, chapter 6 centers on two actual cases, and offers detailed 'to-do' lists of implementation, that can be used both by companies and business institutes and should not be seen as fixed rules. No best practice is transferable, and even best principles are only guidelines. It should be used as a checklist and 'tour guide' to accompany the reader on his journey of creating his own Hybrid Business School, while emphasizing the importance of the learning process that any implementation should entail.

We derived pleasure while doing research for and writing this book, and seeing how the pieces of the jigsaw eventually fell together. Our aim has been to describe a new generation of learning environments in which knowledge management, organizational learning, and individual development are equally important. Supported by the intelligent use of technologies, the IT platforms dynamically create individualized learning solutions for companies that have the courage to allow people to learn, experiment, and develop. Development is an ongoing process, to be initiated by the only one who really knows his needs: the learner himself.

Chapter 1

Economic Environment and Agents of Change

1-1 New Economic Realities

Neither workplace, nor the company, nor the world are even remotely what they were ten years ago. There has never been a time in history when changes have evolved so rapidly, discontinuously, and non-linearly, at the same time affecting countless aspects of everyday and corporate life. Certainly, changes are not novel to history, yet the quantitative and qualitative leaps (flux), and the increase of complexity have never been this intense. As a result, corporate life has become and is becoming more complex, complicated, and paradoxical.

Several economic trends in the world are directly related to the challenges faced within companies today. Trade blocs and free trade zones, deregulation and privatization, a shaky world economy, the opening of emergent countries and markets, the EMU and the introduction of the Euro, the technological interconnectedness of the world – all these things are characteristic of an expansion of the economic environment, yet they make this environment a much 'smaller' marketplace than it used to be.

Deregulation has an increasing impact on competition worldwide. As demonstrated by the telecommunications industry in South America or the airline industry in Europe, however, it is a complicated process. The privatization process of companies such as British Airways or France Telecom demonstrates the difficulty in the shift in 'corporate' focus and cultural change, i.e. the impact of competition, disappearance of state protectionism, and governments slowly backing out of a marketplace where they previously guarded their own interests so heavily. Both opportunities and competition are increasing with the removal of the (quasi) monopolies from many countries. At the same time, there is the emergence of trade blocs in every region of the world, as regions push to safeguard their own interests and protect their own industries from the increasing competition and deregulation which can now reach the far corners of the earth. In other words, we are witnessing a shift from protectionism within a given country to protectionism within a given region, allowing for much greater competition and movement of goods and services.

As borders disappear and markets extend, in global competition, not only do opportunities increase, but so do the number of competitors and the complexity of competition. In how many cases do we really see global competition, as opposed to multi-domestic or cross-national competition? Few products are really global: McDonalds' hamburgers aren't, Boeing's 737 isn't, Ford's Mondeo isn't. Each of these products is tailored to local preferences or specifics. Furthermore, with the rise of technology, distance is no longer a major disincentive to trade, as it is not always necessary to be physically present in a market in order to do business there. Technology also enables 'unconventional' competitors to enter business – unconventional in the sense that a single company or competitor can become a new player in a given field, due to the low cost of the technology. Think about the myriad of small firms specialized in web design. In 1980, 4.5 MIPS (millions of instructions per second) cost about $4.5 million. By 1990, 4.5 MIPS cost about $100.000. It was projected that by the year 2000, this same amount of computer power would cost only $10.000, as indeed it does now. In terms of human resources, this would have equalled 210 people in 1980, and just 0.125 of a person today. The single person in a backroom might be the extreme example, but never before have so many people worked for small companies.

Since the mid-nineties, we have been witnessing another wave of mergers and acquisitions (M&As), joint ventures, alliances and partnerships. Some 32,000 alliances have been formed around the world over the past three years (1995-1998), three quarters of them across borders. Alliances now account for 18% of revenues of America's companies. Particularly in the pharmaceutical, automotive, airline, and financial services industries, companies see growth as their strategy. Alliances come in many shapes and sizes: as joint ventures, minority stakes, co-branding, marketing alliances, co-manufacturing projects, R&D agreements, and so on.

There was also a boom in M&As in the 1980s, but these had a very different strategy. In the eighties, the goal was diversification, whereas recently, the strategy has been to focus on core business, on core competencies, and to look for compatible partners who either add to marketshare (consolidation), have a strong presence in a particular geographical area or a particular market segment, offer compatibility in the value chain, or add the services on which the other partner no longer wishes to focus. Core competencies bundle strategic resources and core technologies, supported by skills, and are harmonized in a governing process. Metaphorically pictured as a tree, the root system is core competence, the trunk is core business, the major limbs are core products, and the leaves, flowers, and fruits are end products.

Underlying to this trend are economies of skill. A good example of this is a June 1998 joint venture in which Psion, Nokia, Ericsson, and Motorola formed a new company called Symbian. Symbian licenses, develops and supports the EPOC operating system – a robust, reliable real time operating system. EPOC has been optimized for Smartphones and Communicators, allowing licensees to design their own user interfaces and select and add relevant applications. This will allow the development of a wide range of compatible devices with different designs and functionality. This joint venture is a very good example of an entity formed by several competitors in the product area, working together in the technology area. Each contributes its own core competencies, and as a whole, the company becomes a powerful entity stimulating innovation.

Finally, there is a considerable increase in socio-political complexities, which directly affect the marketplace and the way business is conducted. The Asian recession and its consequences reach into the far corners of the earth, and also have a grave impact on Western economies. The introduction of the Euro, African and Russian political instability, turmoil in the Middle East, ethnic conflicts in Eastern Europe, the consequences of natural disasters in Central America, and the changing European political environment all contribute to a growing insecurity.

These elements and others, as well as their dynamics and accelerations create new economic realities. This new economic age is presented with a new competitive landscape which is in nature and knows increasing environmental turbulence and uncertainties. Underlying, and in some cases creating these economic trends, is the technological revolution. Technology has changed the shape of the world, the shape of the marketplace, the shape of the company, and the shape of everyday life.

Technological Revolution

Technology enables us to work and live differently. It promotes flexibility in a working environment, allowing people to work from anywhere, without being limited to a certain physical space. This leads to an increase in convenience and to greater productivity of employees, which in general leads to a greater efficiency, less stress, and a happier workforce.

Why go so far as to call it a revolution? One of its most important attributes seems to be radical and dramatic innovations. These innovations, and the high frequency with which they occur, have created the competitive accelerator – shorter and steeper business cycles – making speed a crucial factor in competition. In the late eighties and early nineties, US car manufacturers needed five to seven years to develop and introduce a new model in the market place. Chrysler and the Neon illustrate that US manufacturers understood the importance of development time. Recently, it was announced that Nissan has an eighteen-months' cycle, but Toyota holds the record with fifteen months. In other industries, every 'generation' of new products has to be based on new technology in order to be competitive. Can you imagine now buying a 133Mhz processor computer which not that long ago seemed the high end of the market?

In other words, the technological edge increases constantly, albeit in a discontinuous way – it is not simply a linear movement in time. If we envisage a graph of the past business cycle, it ascends linearly at an angle of 45 degrees. Today's business cycle has steep vertical leaps along the graph and a steeper angle due to the technological developments that speed up the cycle. This means that products have a shorter life cycle, and as a result, they must be marketed much more quickly. Every aspect of the business, however, must become more efficient as competition mounts. Today, to progress at the same rate as the competition means to be running on a treadmill at increasing speed. It is important to remember that to run on a treadmill does not mean companies can afford always to stay in the same place competitively. As the American philosopher Rogers said, even if you are on the right track, you will be run over if you stand still. Speed is not only important, but imperative for those who want to be market leaders.

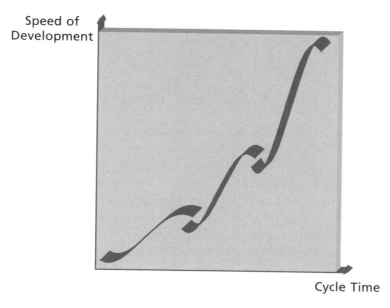

Figure 1.1 The discontinuity of technological developments

The value-adding time factor means that for companies, business value is added by increasing speed, a seemingly simple task. The average competitive advantage a company enjoys due to a particular strategic 'edge' over its competition is about 24 to 28 months. If companies can break this limit and in bringing products to market more quickly, they will reap vast profits. On the other hand, if nothing is done to sustain that competitive edge, then the 24-month period will be the extent of its glory in the marketplace. In order to remain competitive companies must continuously invest in R&D and constantly innovate, while increasing their cycles. Firms must always be learning and developing their core competencies, and must emphasize information and knowledge-building infrastructures. In other words, speed alone is not going to create added value. On the other hand, if everything else in the company is as it should be speed, then the company is likely to get run over and left in the dust.

This all illustrates how technology can modify value activities, transform links in the value chain between stakeholders and even how it enters their value chains. In many cases, the compression of time even underlies the wave of alliances, joint ventures and partnerships.

Collapse of Time

This compression of time is also demonstrated in the increase of modular manufacturing approaches and Just-In-Time systems. Germany's Volkswagen takes it a step further by physically incorporating suppliers in its plants. Suppliers have their own manufacturing units within Volkswagen's manufacturing plant in order to compress the notion of JIT even more. Just-In-Time becomes real time. Portable computers and portable phones allow claims adjusters to make instant decisions, resulting in claims that are settled in minutes rather than weeks or months. Speed saves the insurance company money, it helps customer morale, improves accuracy, lowers prices, and sells. The 'need for speed' illustrates how technology can modify value activities, transform links in the value chain between stakeholders and even how it enters their value chains. In many cases, the compression of time even underlies the wave of alliances, joint ventures and partnerships. More time is spent on reducing time, on shortening horizons. At the same time, an increasing number of executives feel the need to invest more time in the longer-term view, in creating long-term horizons, as they are beginning to understand that instant success takes...time. And as time is a journey of perception, cultural and value-laden patterns carry a great deal of weight in this discussion.

Collapse of Space

As borders disappear, markets extend. In global competition, not only do the opportunities grow, but so do the number of competitors and complexity. Many of these opportunities have been created by world economic development as described earlier. With the advent of technology, distance is no longer a major disincentive to trade. As a result, approximately 95 percent of U.S. business executives have incorporated globalization into their firm's strategy. Implementation seems to be a more difficult issue. In how many cases do we see a truly global approach as opposed to multi-domestic or cross-national approaches? In most cases, companies pursue separate strategies in each of its foreign markets and look at competitive challenges in their individual markets. And again, few products are really global products. From an organizational point of view, globalization has never been further out of reach as companies experience myriads of difficulties in working with their local subsidiaries. Issues such as clashes between local culture and corporate culture, how to offer equal standards of service, dynamics between subsidiaries and corporate headquarters, management of subsidiaries, etcetera, increase distances rather than decrease them.

The Knowledge Era

An important and remarkable development in what today we still call the industrial world is that it is no longer industrial. We are witnessing a rapid transition from an industrial society into a knowledge society. The knowledge society is based on the growing importance of knowledge as the so-called fourth production factor. Many products and certainly all services have high research and development costs, whereas the actual production costs are fairly low. Developing and launching a new operating system like Windows represents a big investment for Microsoft, which makes the first copy very expensive, but any further copies relatively cheap.

Employing a number of consultants is a large investment for a consulting company, but when they are actively working on a project, the costs are virtually zero. Having the knowledge base, which means having the consultants available, is expensive. To have them actually working for a client, however, is relatively cheap. Even car manufacturing, the best example of industrial production in the Western world has become increasingly knowledge-based. Over 40% of the sales price of a car stems from research, development and marketing.

We still talk about the industrialized countries, since most of our thinking is still based on concepts of industrial production dating back to the earlier parts of this century. What we have observed, though, is that increasingly, companies are beginning to optimize supply chains and that those supply chains evolve into demand and supply chains. The following step consists of having those chains supported with information technology (IT) in order to increase their efficiency. Strangely enough, in a next stage, a progressive use of IT puts pressure on the very existence of the chain. The more the integration of a chain has been based on IT, the greater the pressure that is created, making the chain explode into a network. In these circumstances especially, it is the owner of the knowledge base that manages the process. Network structures evolve around knowledge centers. Companies manage brands and outsource most of the chain itself. Extreme examples of this approach are probably Calvin Klein, Benetton and Nike. Again, knowledge, and especially the ability to manage, create and share knowledge, is becoming the focussing point for the successful company. Via brand management and direct marketing, this can be translated to, for instance, targeted clients. This is the visible part of the transformation of an industrial market into a knowledge-based market. In this way, knowledge becomes yet another attribute of the changing economic reality.

In a company, knowledge can take different shapes. It can be divided into three categories. Tacit knowledge is mainly based on lived experiences while explicit knowledge refers to the rules and procedures that are followed by a company. Cultural knowledge, then, is the environment in which the company and the individuals employed by the company operate.

Different forms of knowledge come into existence as a result of different activities. Conversion of knowledge occurs because of the tacit and explicit knowledge that a person possesses or has access to. Knowledge is very often created during joint work sessions, such as brainstorms, management meetings, etcetera. Equally important but more difficult to capture is knowledge processing via assimilation. Very often, assimilation has cultural knowledge as a first input, which is then reinforced by tacit knowledge that quite often collapses as a result of explicit rules. It is important to stress, however, that knowledge management is merely the 'sufficient' condition. The 'necessary' condition needed to deal with new economic realities are the boundary conditions of knowledge management. Together, this is the learning culture of a company.

Above all, knowledge management and learning represent an attitude and a way of working with management. They are overall approaches that go beyond functional tactics. One could even say that knowledge management is a kind of philosophy of management rather than a science. This process is one of redefining a company's aims from a profit-making or share-value increasing entity to a knowledge-creating unit. The profit-making organization has a rather short-term focus, whereas the knowledge-creating type has a more visionary and long-term one.

The aim of the company is no longer purely growth as such, but rather sustainable development and renewal. Hence, organizations not only need knowledge, they also need the skills and competence in order to dynamically update and to put their knowledge into practice. To be able to do this, organizations need to be in a continuous learning process and need to use the acquired knowledge for improvement. Hence, organizations should embrace the philosophy of the learning organization, and the process of organizational learning.

A learning organization enables each of its members to learn constantly and helps to generate new ideas and thinking. Thus, organizations continuously learn from their own experiences and those of others, in this way increasing their efficiency towards the achievement of their goal. In a way, learning organizations aim to convert

themselves into 'knowledge-based' organizations by creating, acquiring and transferring knowledge in order to improve their planning as well as their activities.

In order to build a learning organization, or a corporate learning
culture, companies should be skilled at systematic problem solving,
learning from their own experience, learning from the experiences
of others, processing knowledge quickly and efficiently within their
organization, and experimenting with new approaches. Developments in information and knowledge technologies make it increasingly possible to achieve these competitive needs and skills.

1-2 Complex Dynamic Behavior

In the previous section, we described the agents of change within
new economic realities. It becomes apparent that managerial complexity is not only on the increase, it is also changing. On the one
hand, a higher degree of complexity in management as well as dissi-
pating structures force companies into quantitative and qualitative
leaps of improvement. On the other hand, due to a faster rate of
change and a greater velocity in the world economy, some changes
are becoming more apparent. When studying today's market behavior, we can no longer speak of an objective world where interactions
can be described in linear terms, where words have single meanings,
and where prognosis and control are paramount.

In the past, notably so when market changes were slower, we became used to thinking in terms of reasonably linear behavior; after
all, markets and industries appeared to be fairly stable or mature. It
was thought future behavior could be easily predicted by means of
past observations, and in many respects we developed complex
methods to extrapolate linear trends. However, in reality, markets
do and did not behave in a linear way. The future is not a simple
extrapolation of the past. A given action can lead to several possible
outcomes ('futures'), some of which are disproportionate in size to
the action itself. The 'whole' is therefore not equal to the sum of the
'parts'. This contrasting perspective evolved from complexity and
chaos theory. Complexity theory challenges the traditional man-

agement assumptions by embracing non-linear and dynamic behavior of systems, and by the belief that human activity allows for the possibility of emergent behavior. Emergence can be defined as the overall system behavior that stems from the interaction of many participants – behavior that cannot be predicted or even culled from the knowledge about the behavior of each component of a system. Organizations, for example, often see processes of change as emergent behavior. Complexity theory also tells corporate executives that beyond a certain point, increased knowledge of complex, dynamic systems does little to improve the ability to extend the horizon of predictability for those systems. No matter how much one knows about the weather, no matter how powerful one's computers, specific long-range predictions are impossible. With only knowledge and no predictions there can be no certainty.

The focus on non-linear behavior of markets collides with the traditional positivist and Cartesian view of the world. That positivist perspective, translated into traditional management literature – the stuff that most MBAs are taught – describes 'the' world in terms of variables and matrices, and as existing within a certain system of coordinates. Exact and objective numbers are needed in order to create models, while simulations can offer a 'correct' picture of what to expect. Particularly business schools have welcomed this 'scientific' way of dealing with management problems as being the one that could bring business schools on a par with the 'scientific' level of the sciences. It is clear that much of existing management practice, theory, and 'remedies' based on the positivist view are limited by their dependence on several inappropriate assumptions – they do not reflect business and market behavior. In business schools, linear and static methods are taught. Therefore, markets are concluded to be linear and static – as we know they are not.

It is important to elaborate a little on positivist thinking as later, we will propose a challenging view on management and management education. In order to do this, we will briefly look at some positivist epistemology. Epistemology is concerned with understanding the origin, nature and validity of knowledge, i.e., the science or theory of – in our case – positivism. These fundamental assumptions that are into the epistemological outlook play a vital role in determining practices regarding management, organization, and knowledge.

A major aspect of positivism is the division between object and subject. This means that the outer world – e.g. an industry – is a given, ready to be 'truthfully' represented by organizations and individuals. The mind is able to create an inner representation that corresponds to the outer world, be it an object, event, or state. Translated into knowledge, positivism takes knowledge to exist independently of the human being that uses it, integrates it, transfers it. Knowledge reflects and represents 'the world in itself' and can be constructed independently of the observer, the 'knower'. This is equally and arguably the basis for most management education today. A student, irrespective of his background, interests, social environment, ambitions etcetera, needs to learn a quantity of knowledge by means of courses and is tested on whether that 'objective' knowledge has been acquired. However, the professor who judges is subjective and is involved in the subject matter. The way one professor teaches is different from the way another teaches so, the content is in fact subject-dependent. We call it 'subject matter', even though we consider it to be an objective quantity of transferable knowledge. The more companies want to tailor management education to their specific needs – based on their employees' previous knowledge – the more this positivist object/subject division becomes a problem as it collides with the notion of 'universal and objective' knowledge. What if the universal knowledge that is transferred is mainly a theoretical framework, which is of little use in non-linear and dynamic markets? This would mean management education does not prepare adequately for managerial reality.

As is argued in chapter 3, individualized learning needs an adapted pedagogical approach, which enables dynamic and non-linear behavior. The successful implementation of the concept of the Hybrid Business School is not based on a positivist and reductionist view on management education.

Another premise of positivist thinking is based on a strict belief in (absolute) causality and (environmental) determinism. As there exist clear-cut connections between cause and effect, managerial actions lead to predictable outcomes and thus to control. Because of negative feedback processess, successful systems can be driven toward predictable states of adaptation to the environment. The dynamics of success are therefore assumed to be a tendency towards stability, regularity, and predictability. This reductionism is illustrated by the classic approach to strategy. The complexities of industries are reduced to terms of maturity, continuity and stability so that a single prediction of an organization's future path can be made. As a consequence, the better the environmental analysis, the better the course (strategy) can be defined and implemented.

Positivism is the prevailing scientific view in the Western world, since it perfectly coincides with the Cartesian view of the world: the over-riding power of man where it concerns nature. Nature gives man the power to master nature, according to laws of nature. In 1903, however, Poincaré, a French mathematician, began to question this positivist view. Without really having any proof, he warned:

> 'Sometimes, small differences in the initial conditions generate very large differences in the final phenomena. A slight error in the former could produce a tremendous error in the latter. Prediction becomes impossible; we have accidental phenomena.'

It suggested that with existing approaches, man was not always able to control his own systems. Hence, this spelled the end to the Cartesian view of the world.

Quite a number of years later, in 1964, Lorenz, an American meteorologist, evidence of the phenomenon. Lorenz was interested in weather forecasting. In order to produce forecasts, he built a simple dynamic non-linear model. Though it only consisted of a few equations and a few variables, it showed 'strange' behavior. A dynamic model is one where the value in a given period is a function of the value in the previous period. For example, the value of a particular price in a given period is a function of its value in the previous period. Or, the market share for product A in a given period is a function of the market share in the previous period. In other words, most, if not all, economic phenomena are dynamic. Such a dynamic, continuously changing can only be simulated by a procedure consisting of very small incremental steps, and is an iterative process. Once the value of the previous period has been calculated, it is used as an input value for the next period, etcetera.

A computer allowed Lorenz to show what could happen with non-linear dynamic systems. At a certain point, he interrupted a simulation, since he needed to leave the room. He requested a printout of the simulation. When he returned, he decided not to start the entire simulation from scratch, but rather to start where he had stopped before. In order to be sure, he re-started the simulation with an earlier period. What he observed was remarkable: the new simulation differed considerably from the one made previously; also, the differences increased over time. Suddenly, chaos seemed to appear. The observed difference became larger than the signal itself. Hence, the predictive value of the model became zero.

Originally, Lorenz did not understand what happened. He did observe that while the computer calculated with a number of decimal positions, the printout showed fewer decimal positions. When he started the re-simulation, he typed in the value of the output, which differed slighter (from the ninth decimal position onwards) from the one the computer really used during the simulations. After a number of iterations, this tiny difference resulted in chaotic behavior. Lorenz' observation caused a real paradigm shift in sciences. Lorenz proved what Poincaré suggested, namely that non-linear dynamic systems are highly sensitive to initial conditions. Complex adaptive systems are probabilistic rather than deterministic, and factors such as non-linearity can magnify apparently insignificant differences in initial conditions into huge consequences, meaning that the long term outcomes for complex systems are unknowable. Translated into management terms, this suggests strongly that companies and economies need to be encouraged to embraces flux and competition in complex and chaotic contexts rather than to embrace a rational approach. Mainstream approaches that are popular in business texts, however, seldom come to grips with non-linear phenomena. Instead, they tend to model phenomena as if they were linear in order to make them tractable and controllable, and tend to model aggregate behavior as if it is produced by individual entities which all exhibit average behavior.

One could ask what this has to do with education. The answer is quite simple. Human beings behave and think in a non-linear and dynamic way. Each individual, even when from the same region and having benefitted from the same pre-education as another, thinks differently from his or her colleagues. Therefore, a particular course can never fit all students. Furthermore, it is extremely difficult to identify the 'initial conditions' of each student. This failing where it concerns initial conditions is another reason for investigating new educational paradigms. The old paradigm no longer fits the modern world.

Positive feedback has been brought into the realm of economics by Brian Arthur, who claims that there are really two economies, one that functions on the basis of traditional diminishing returns, and one where, due to positive feedback, increasing returns to scale are evident. Marshall introduced the concept of diminishing returns as early as 1890. This theory was based on industrial production, where one could chose out of many resources, and relatively little knowledge was involved in production. Production then seemed to follow the law of diminishing returns, based on negative feedback in the process, leading to a unique market equilibrium. Arthur's second economy includes most knowledge industries. In the knowledge economy, companies should focus on adapting themselves, recognizing patterns, and building networks to amplify positive feedback rather than trying to achieve 'optimal' performance. A good example is VHS becoming a market standard, without being technically superior. When the video became popular, there were at least two standards on the market, Betamax, which was technically better, and VHS. Initially, both were present on the market, and neither was dominant. At a certain point, some video producers decided to use VHS standard for the majority of movies. Obviously, this led to more equipment manufacturers to choose for, which in turn led to more movie producers using VHS. A snowball effect ensued, which made VHS the market leader, even though Betamax offered better technology at a comparable price.

Brian Arthur also refers to the American pre-elections as another example of this 'positive feedback phenomena'. All presidential candidates make a great effort to conquer the very first small yet crucial states, such as New Hampshire. This is not because it gains them a lot of votes, but rather because it is known that the candidate who wins these states over will get more campaign funding, more TV time, etcetera. Those who lose often get into a downward spiral and soon afterwards drop out. American presidents, says

Brian Arthur, are not elected by a majority of American citizens, but rather by those living in a few small states.

Arthur also specified a number of reasons for the increasing returns that particularly fits today's economy; most products, as they are highly knowledge-intensive, with high up-front costs, network effects, and customer relationships, lead to complex customer behavior. Again, let us take the example of Windows. The first version of Windows is quite expensive due to huge research costs; as a result, Microsoft will experience a loss on the first generation. The second and following generations however, cost relatively little, but the revenue per product remains the same. Hence, there is a process of increasing returns.

Two more interesting developments have consequences for our educational practice. Recent neurobiological research, e.g. by Varela, has led to the concept of self-organization and the concept that knowledge is not stored, but rather created over and again, based on the neural capacity of the brain. Cognition is enacted, which means that cognition only exists in action and interpretation. This concept of enacted cognition goes fundamentally against the prevailing idea that objects are outside and the brain is inside the person. The subject can be considered to be the special experience of oneself, as a process in terms of truth. By identifying with objects, the individual enables objects to 'talk' to him. In other words, subject and object meet in interaction, in hybrid structures. Individuals thus become builders of facts in constructing contents of knowledge which relate to events, occurrences and states. Knowledge is concerned with the way one learns to fix the flow of the world in temporal and spatial terms. Consequently, claims of truth are transposed on objects; the subject is 'de-subjectivized'. There is no such subdivision between the object and the subject. Cognition is produced by an embodied mind, a mind that is part of a body, sensors and an environment. This issue will also be dealt with in chapter 2, when we focus on the role of managers, and in chapter 5, when we discuss education, and again in particular assessment issues.

Research in an artificial context provided us with the insight that, instead of reducing the complex world to simple simulation models which are never correct, one could equally define some simple rules, which then produce complex behavior. This is also a form of self-organization, like a flock of birds that flies south. The first bird is not the leader and does not command the flock. Rather, each bird abides by a simple rule, e.g. to stay 20 cm away from its two neighbors. This simple rule allows us to simulate the complex behavior of a flock of birds.

At this stage we will focus on what is understood by complex behavior. Complex systems behavior is the behavior of non-linear dynamic systems. A system is dynamic if the value in a given period – say, today – would depend on the value of the previous period. A non-linear system is a system in which the evolution of the phenomenon does not take place by adding elements to each period, but rather by multiplying them. A simple example: consider waterplants on a lake. It is said that in a given period, the surface covered by them doubles. That means that each period of time, the surface is multiplied by two. Over a number of periods t, the surface can be calculated by 2^t. This is an example of a system which is at the same time dynamic and non-linear. It is dynamic since the surface covered in period t is a function of the surface covered in previous period (times two); it is non-linear since in each period, a multiplication takes place and not an addition. In the end, this will lead to an exponential formula.

Probabilistic, non-linear dynamic systems are still considered to be deterministic. That means that such systems follow rules, even if these are difficult to identify and even if the appearance of the simulated phenomenon suggests complete chaos. At different times, the same complex system can produce chaotic or orderly behavior. The change between chaos and order cannot be forecast, nor can the moment in which it will take places, either in magnitude or direction. Complexity and chaos refer to the state of a system and not to something complicated, i.e., something that is difficult to do. The latter depends not on the system, but more on the environment and boundary conditions. For instance, for a handicapped person, driving a car is probably more complicated. In general, building a house seems more complicated than sewing a suit, but for some people building a house would be less complicated than it would be to sew a suit. This depends on the boundary conditions for each individual person.

To formalize the findings of complexity theory in a simplified way, we could list three characteristics. First, complex systems are highly dependent on the initial state. A slight change in the starting situation can have dramatic consequences in a later period of time caused by the dynamic and iterative character of the system. Second, one cannot forecast the future based on the past. Based on the irreversibility of the time principle, one can only make one step at a time, while scanning carefully the new starting position. Third, the scaling factor of a non-linear system causes the appearance of 'strange attractors', a local minimum or maximum which, in quasi equilibrium, a system seems adhere to for a certain period of time. The number of attractors cannot be forecasted, and neither can it be forecasted when they will attract the phenomenon.

We can gain a myriad of insights from complexity theory and its applications to business and markets for management education in order to better organize the Hybrid Business School around complex markets and behavior. The strength of the self-organizing ability of the individual and of groups of people forces us to change the focus of education. Instead of school-centered, education will become learner-centered. The learner decides, chooses and manages, based on what he or she needs for his/her learning purposes, at that particular moment, and in that particular situation, based on the abilities of that particular individual. The concept of enacted cognition invites us to redefine management education in the direction of learning by doing. Project-based education and competency-based education are two focuses that need to be incorporated into the concept of the Hybrid Business School. The concept of the embodied mind stresses the need to learn within a given context. Management education, certainly if organized by the company itself, should be grounded in the corporate effort in knowledge management. One can only learn efficiently within one's own context. Learning is not value free; there is no division between object and subject. Management education can only take place within the managerial context, which should be integrated and not divided into functional areas.

The 'irreversibility of time' theorem suggests that there is no best solution. There are 'best' principles that can be used to learn, but no best solutions or practices that one could copy. Indeed, there are no guaranteed solutions that can be used in most circumstances. This fact points to the need for a different way of organizing the pedagogical process of learning, as we should accept that no theories are universal in management education.

Recent developments within complexity theory suggest that management education should be based on an integrated, holistic approach and not on a reductionist, rationalist paradigm. Many interesting but complex challenges arise when management education is seen as a useful tool for companies operating in non-linear dynamic markets. And essentially, this means *all* companies. The concept of the Hybrid Business School that will be developed in the course of this book, will describe an approach to the design of management education and management development that supports both companies and managers in dynamic and non-linear markets on an operational level.

1-3 Building Stones for the Hybrid Business School

- The high frequency with which radical and dramatic innovations occur have created a competitive accelerator and steeper business cycles, making time and speed crucial factors in remaining competitive and in forcing companies into quantitative and qualitative leaps of improvement;
- A rapid transition is taking place which is turning our industrial society into a knowledge society.

References

- Arthur, B. (1990). *Positive Feedbacks in the Economy. Scientific American*, February 1999, pp. 92-99.
- Baets, W. (1998). *Organizational Learning and Knowledge Technologies in a Dynamic Environment.* Kluwer Academic Publishers.
- Baets, W. & Galliers, B. (1998). *IT and Organisational Transformation.* Wiley.
- Baets, W., ed. (1999). *A Collection of Essays on Complexity and Management.* Singapore, New York: World Scientific.
- Cohen, J. & Stewart, I. (1994). *The Collapse of Chaos: Discovering Simplicity in a Complex World.*
- Maturana, H. & Varela, F. (1984). *The Tree of Knowledge: The Biological Roots of Human Understanding.* Scherz Verlag.
- McKenna, R. (1997). *Real Time: Preparing for the Age of the Never-Satisfied Customer.* Boston, MA.: Harvard Business School Publishing.
- Nicolis, G. & Prigogine, I. (1989). *Exploring Complexity.* Freeman.
- Prigogine, I. & Stengers, I. (1988). *Entre le Temps et L'éternité.* Fayard.
- Stewart, I. (1989). *Does God Play Dice: The Mathematics of Chaos.* Blackwell.
- Waldrop, M. M. (1992). *Complexity.* London: Penguin Books.

Chapter 2

Corporate Environment

2-1 Changing Managerial Roles and Management Competencies

In this chapter, we will discuss the impact of new economic realities, the technological revolution and other agents of change in organizations, organizational processes, and how this impact is consequently incorporated into the role of managers, managerial processes, and management as such. Furthermore, we will look into the issue of management competencies. What are management competencies, how are they defined, and what are the important management competencies that can be identified in the context of changing corporate and business environments?

Changing Managerial Roles and Mindsets

Companies are preparing themselves for more competition and more varied forms of competitive pressure from international, knowledge-rich, and unconventional rivals. Key factors are rapid moves onto new markets, extreme flexibility, and gauging the weight of competitors. Even organizations in slow-moving industries are suddenly faced with threats from more active and internet-based competitors. Other companies have seen such drastic changes in their industry's structure that they need to develop a completely new outlook in order not to become obsolete.

A logical starting point is to look into and assess the key factors, which will drive competitive advantage in the future. According to a recent survey of the Economist's Intelligence Unit, companies will have to focus strongly on relationships with suppliers and customers, human capital/human resources, core competencies, capabilities and strategic resources, flexible organizational structures, high productivity, technology and low-cost production. These issues will be defining the hallmark of competitive advantage for the next ten years, thus forcing forms to achieve a flexible and sound strategy.

Companies are trying to maximize their core competencies, strategic resources and skills by looking to and relying on partners to perform certain activities in the value chain. Core competencies combine strategic resources and core technologies, and are supported by skills and harmonized in a governing process. They reflect the ability to create new businesses, core products, end products and services by adapting skills and innovative use of resources rather than by fixing a few core competencies. Metaphorically pictured as a tree, the root system is core competence, the trunk is core business, the main branches are core products, and the leaves, flowers, and fruits are end products. The idea of referring to organizations as portfolios of core competencies stresses dispersion and fragmentation. At the same time, firms are looking for new competitive advantages beyond their core competencies and strategic resources. Besides the diffusion of innovation in the marketplace, the importance of drastic innovation, and the increasing emphasis on the design of new products and marketing them rapidly also play an important role in this process.

Increasingly, we see the birth of role organizations within a federal model, i.e., networked organizations within a consortium or conglomerate. The Italian fashion company Benetton and the luxury brand Gucci are built around such a model. Benetton, for example, is organized around two networks led by a strong central authority. One consists of hundreds of small textile firms while, the other is based on thousands of retail franchises around the world. Gucci, on the other hand, is a network organization of about seventy small handicraft firms. Every so often, a certain number of such firms are enabled to join the existing group on the basis of reliable quality. Central to Gucci's organization is its buying and cutting department. The company has also remained owner of its distribution network.

These days, joint ventures, alliances, outsourcing, and cooperation within industries are popular ways to create such flexible structures.

The results are great interdependence as well as expectations. Firms have to create facilitating, coordinating and cooperative mechanisms in order to promote use and enhancement of their new partners' knowledge-intensive competencies. Constantly changing processes, continuous adaptation of new skills in order to retain that competitive edge, continuous recreation of specific business-related capacities as well as changing structures in industry: all these factors make us new organizations as diverse, decentralized, process and flow-oriented entities. As such, twenty-first century firms are constantly engaged in boundary busting, as internal networks overflow into external networks and vice versa. This not only makes it difficult to draw clear and objective topological boundaries between an organization and its environment, but the fragmenting impact of these firms cause their employees to view them and their environments as complicated, turbulent, chaotic, antagonistic, complex, and ambiguous realities.

Because of these fragmentations, managers no longer hold a unique position in today's organizations. Almost everyone can be considered to be a manager in the traditional sense, even the secretary/ executive assistant, who must possess a sophisticated level of communication as well as professional skills. Strategic leadership, that was typically part of the traditional management role, for example, is much more widely distributed than ever before. The company's systems are in the hands not of senior executives, but of lower-tier workers. Secretaries or administrative assistants decide with whom their immediate supervisors should communicate, and on what subjects, as there is much information which needs to be intellectually processed for it to all be 'important enough' to pass on.

Managers increasingly realize that they themselves are subject and object in/of these turbulent networks and information flows. As a result, they can not escape the complexities they are confronted with. And we are not talking 'big' strategic issues, but also phenomena managers experience on a day-to-day basis. They turn into paradoxes which perplex many a manager. Many of them have the feeling that they are loosing control, that they are no longer 'managing to manage the complexity'. In the previous chapters, we have tried to come to a deeper understanding of business and of organizational life. Moreover, our discussions about complexity have shown that it is impossible to control complexity, as it is a dynamic and non-linear reality. Hence, we could say that we are on the verge of a new managerial mindset that can take advantage of this rich complexity, and which concentrates on managing complexities rather than to 'manage to manage the complexities'.

To illustrate this new managerial mindset or philosophy, we would like to use the analogy with Pirsig's *Zen and the Art of Motorcycle Maintenance*. In much detail and in a readable way, Pirsig describes the attitude that we refer to in this book. He argues for an open mind about the outside world and the tools with which we work. The book advocates really listening and reflecting on possible evidence, rather than using the automatic pilot mechanism. It argues strongly against an attitude that has become common in many companies: managers need to know answers to all questions, and if they do not, then they are bad managers. Pirsig, on the other hand, promotes a managerial philosophy, and introduces the conditions for knowledge management. Managers should manage as if they were part of the environment. It is like driving a car. When a person drives a car, he looks at nature through a window. Nature passes by as if the driver was looking at it on a tv screen, while seated in his chair. The driver is not part of the environment. Nature becomes distant and we do not really have any feeling for it any longer. In the same way, management becomes a movie that we are watching. On a motorbike, however, Pirsig argues, the driver is part of nature. He feels and smells nature and is able to react much faster to changes in nature. This analogy suggests that managers should be more in touch with their surroundings – riding their bike – in order to get a feel for the state of the markets, for how their employees work, and for other stakeholders' motives. They should learn and share their experiences rather than stay in their offices, looking at the world as if they were looking at a tv screen.

Managers should not operate on their automatic pilot, but instead remain attentive to any minor changes that could snowball at a later stage. Self-criticism is a quality that many managers lack, as they think they have experienced it all and immediately jump to conclusions. Perhaps reality is 'slightly' different. It holds within it a dynamic movement that can grow very fast. Hence, managers should pay attention to their surroundings and remain alert in order to be able to react. When we have seen, we can start to learn and know.

Instead of over-emphasizing procedures and rules, people should be enabled to enjoy in their jobs. Procedures, rules, or processes do not offer the answer; but people who share experiences create knowledge. When people enjoy their jobs, they identify with the job and put their soul into it. They will want to learn and to adapt since they do not feel threatened by rules and regulations but are free to come up with an idea or a proposal. They will start paying attention to detail since they will observe things they have not seen before and will enjoy it. An eye for detail is the basic attitude for quality improvement. Furthermore, quality is also the ability to really listen to problems. By identifying with underlying signifiers, these signifiers are enabled to 'talk', to tell their 'story'. Managers should therefore take time in order to be able to take critical distance. Let us paraphrase Pirsig to clarify this point:

"The motorbike broke down and I knew I had not checked it over carefully enough. I had presumed that it was the rain that had caused the engine to fail. Perhaps what I should have done was just take a step away from the bike, take a good long look at it and attempt to listen to it. Allow it to work on you a while, just the way you would go fishing. You stare at the float and after a while you catch a fish. If you give it the time and the space, and allow it to happen, you will detect some almost imperceptible movement or detail that will attract your attention. And that's what makes the world go round: attention."

If one 'listens' to the managerial or organizational phenomenon, often the phenomenon itself suggests solutions. Critical distance and reflection – slowing down the thinking process in order to become more aware – make individuals think about issues, find limitations, and develop an epistemology of inquiry – holding dialogues and developing knowledge about assumptions – that allows them to contribute to the knowledge base by asking the pertinent questions. Working on management is working on oneself. In this way, quality will come to mean a healthy combination of man and machine, and thus knowledge management will come to mean a healthy combination of a learning culture and an information and knowledge technology based network.

As Pirsig shows, managers should not try to find *the* answer to every issue. Trying to find answers to problems about organizational issues will only turn into problems about answers. Managerial life consists of perplexing paradoxes. These paradoxes portray a confusion or collapse of different logical levels. Even though contradictions are inferred, they are not merely referring to a simple contradiction. Paradoxes suppose *con-fusion*: the different levels cannot be reached because the fusion causes the differentiation of logical levels to disappear. This makes clear why in managerial life the 'and ... and' prevails over the 'or ... or'. It is the 'genius of the and' dominating the 'tyranny of the or'. The answer is not a choice between two elements. 'Or' does not lie in two opposing extremes. Travelling between tensions and using those tensions allows a search for openings that make new choices possible. This is the 'core' competency of the manager. By using and reconciling tensions, by taking critical distance, managers become 'agents in realities'. Making sense of paradoxes is a powerful vehicle since they represent an intellectual and philosophical context; they say something about the actor, the action and the acting fields. It is by means of this movement and continuous transformation that paradoxes are expressed.

Management has a clear rhetorical function. It produces new realities, new meaningful contexts which each have their own particular 'grammar'. One could say it is the manager's role to identify temporally shared elements within a complex entity, to identify unity in diversity and diversity in unity while attempting to translate dynamic interactions into the moment. The management of meanings should be approached as a strategic journey. The manager's interest in meanings and knowledge starts from a time perspective. In this way, advantage can be taken of the richness of complexity and flux. Knowledge is exactly concerned with what one learns in the process of translating (giving meaning to) the flow of his world and involvement in contexts. Hence, management is a mindset to be understood as a continuous movement without location. It is differing in space and deferring in time.

Management Competencies

The fragmented and discontinuous nature of a manager's job and the constant bombardment with information and meetings cause managers to behave in a non-systematic fashion. Also, no single concept of management captures the diversity of roles and activities that are the manager's. As executives live in and create complex corporate environments, they will have to command a whole set of personal skills in order to excel. What is becoming prevalent in management is the need for multi-faceted knowledge, intelligence, and competencies needed to create progress – i.e., having a flexible strategic vision and constantly renewing, while preserving the organization's core (Collins & Porras' 'clock building'). Competencies refer to the capacity of creating new businesses, core competencies, skills, products and services. It emphasizes individuals' ability to learn about the environment, about their own performance, their objectives and skills, and, in the light of this learning, to change, and to learn from the change. Indeed, state-of-the-art competencies are sustained by constant learning, as though they were a genetic sequence of evolutions.

In a broader sense, competencies are not only relevant from the manager's standpoint, but also from that of the organization. In project-based high-tech firms and flat or networked companies, it is especially important to increase employability through developing competencies. Increasing employability and personal development is one way of compensating for the lack of vertical promotion.

Which are the relevant managerial competencies, given the new managerial mindset? Discussing competencies enables one to avoid the muddle of traits and motives that are attributed to (in this case) a manager's role. Unlike the word 'characteristics' which refers to the whole person, 'competency' refers to performance. In other words, it is role, context, and person-related. On the other hand, according to Woodruffe, talking about competencies is like entering a minefield. Numerous lists exist with 'crucial' competencies and a myriad of competency-models, making the whole issue of 'competency' an enigma. Competencies have something intangible, something of an illusion. Besides, the term 'competency' is used by different people to mean different things. Consequently, different models portray different things.

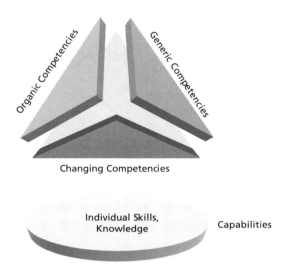

Changing Competencies

Individual Skills, Knowledge   Capabilities

Figure 2.1 Managerial competency model

According to us, the essence of managerial competencies is in the managerial mindset, which reflects an epistemology. An epistemology defines knowledge, methods, and their limitations. In analogy with the notion of core competencies, managerial competencies combine strategic resources and intellectual technologies that underlie managerial roles and practices, and processes for understanding, connecting and exploiting these competencies in a uniquely competitive way. Recombining resources and technologies will be especially important to managers.

Managerial competencies are supported by capabilities. Capabilities describe for instance the behavioral skills needed to communicate, to work in a team, and to understand the dynamics of the work context of individual managers. An important personal development can be triggered by the changing capabilities.

In order to clarify the different aspects of managerial roles, i.e., having to deal with fragmentation and perplexing paradoxes as well as with daily routines, we will distinguish between the following categories: generic, organic and changing competencies. The symbiosis between these three articulates the manager's perplexities: how to arrive at a deeper understanding of networking and vision, how to avoid ambiguity, how to handle high complexity and labyrinths of meanings, as well as individuals and turbulent issues. Once the different competency dimensions have been defined, each competency has to be translated into observable, behavioral facts. Also, competencies must be divided into key output areas that can each be allocated relative importance.

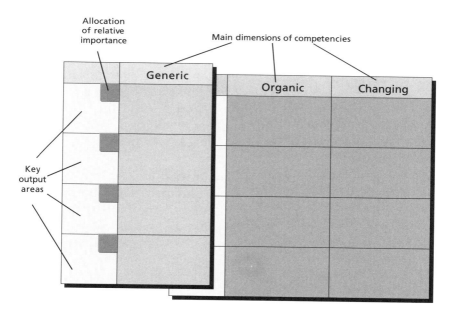

Figure 2.2 Competency table

First, there are 'generic or transferable' competencies. These competencies can be applied to managers in a range of organizations and roles. Existing in varying degrees of importance, they refer to the more abstract competencies, to an epistemology of inquiry reflecting thought processes and critical distance. Epistemology is concerned with understanding the origin, nature and validity of knowledge, i.e., the theory of (in this case) inquiry. Generic competencies can be used by a range of managers, as they are at the heart of the managerial mindset, of managerial and organizational life. A few examples of this category are critical distance, understanding paradoxes, and the ability to really listen. Other examples could include a customer-friendly attitude and cross-functional respect. The latter two could be respectively described as being open to the customer's changing needs, and respect for other functions' responsibilities and ambitions.

Next, we can distinguish 'organic' competencies. Organic competencies are role-specific. From a more traditional perspective, these competencies would be referred to as job-related. In a broader sense, they be derived from a specific company's business strategy, as well as its core competencies, skills, culture, values, and vision. Managers need to look for patterns that lurk beneath seemingly random behavior and only 'organic' competencies are specific and fluid enough to represent categories of certain types of managerial work or roles and organizational contexts. In that sense, they are discontinuous. Technical leadership, problem solving and project management are some illustrations of organic competencies.

Third, 'changing competencies' are forward-looking and related to the lifecycle of competencies. As we said earlier, it is crucial not to start with just a few competencies, but to recombine resources and technologies, to evolve changing skills. These time-related competencies do just that, connecting speed to strategic purposes, information, critical issues, and knowledge management. It includes emerging, transitional, and maturing competencies, which refer to those competencies that have an increasing relevance and importance for the next few years (emerging), the competencies whose relevance gradually decreases (maturing), or competencies whose relevance may decrease while their present emphasis remains (transitional). Competencies related to technology changing competencies, due to the constantly changing nature of technology. Another example would be competencies related to business development.

The obvious challenge, then, will be to ensure that these competencies will become sufficiently embedded into the organization's every practice as well as its learning process. 'Sufficiently embedded' implies a consciously learned phenomenon, as opposed to an assumption of understanding. Hence, it can be concluded that many senior level managers *think* they have excellent leadership and managerial competencies, but without any real foundation. Because it is deemed necessary for all people in a managerial position to be professionally taught leadership, development programs have to ensure that the skills and knowledge they teach are truly alive. Managerial and leadership competencies such as networking, vision, strategic attention to information, are all needed for coordination and organizational dynamics, production of implicit knowledge and core capabilities, and consistency with corporate strategies. As will be shown later, it requires a complete educational approach to be able to incorporate competencies into development programs. Actually, competencies are one of the important agents in the alliance between companies and providers of management education. As we will see in chapters 5 and 6, the competency approach will be one of the hybrid business school's main elements of added value.

2-2 Information as a Dynamic Process

The impact of the new economy on companies and work has so far been quite complex. It has affected organizational processes as well as organizational design, the nature of competition, products and services.

Basically, the economy has progressed from the industrial age to the information age, i.e., from physical sources to knowledge sources. Although physical sources are an important aspect of the economy, true value nowadays lies in information, learning, and knowledge management. Information and knowledge are greatly underestimated and underutilized, even though the formal process of acquiring and using it effectively is becoming more widespread.

As an example, let us consider manufacturing, in which one can observe a shift from physical resources to information resources. In other words, manufacturing is becoming less dependent on materials. Think about the beer can, which originally weighed .66 ounces – half the weight of a steel one. Now it weighs about .48 ounces. The gain here is in information, in the manufacturing process, in information of chemical engineering. Products thrive on more information. Over half the cost of finding and extracting petroleum lies in information. The BMW 700 series needs more computer power than the Apollo 11 that landed on the moon. The value of all chips produced today exceeds the value of the total production of steel. Market intelligence and information about the customer are increasingly important factors in achieving customer loyalty. Hence, the new information economy is transforming the old industrial economy and reducing its relative importance.

How should we look at information? Is it just data that can be stored in databases? The importance of information stems not necessarily from its value and scarcity, but rather from a lack of knowledge on how to extract and exploit what information from the marketplace, as information is often free, but not freely accessible or available. A simple example of this is a search on the web. Person A may enter some key words in an attempt to find information (assuming he knows what his optimal information would be for a given situation), and comes up with nothing. Person B enters his key words, and soon has all the information he thinks he needs. Person B has an 'information advantage'.

The price of information does not reflect its value. Meaning, usefulness, and value of information are intertwined. Particular information is useful to a person in a particular context, because it has a particular meaning. For another person, that same information will have a different meaning or usefulness, hence for that person it has a different value or price. The well-known Sabre system that provides information about travelers is a good example. American Airlines, the owner of the system, sells this information to many companies who use the information for various purposes.

Furthermore, as a result of the collapse of space and time, information and its nature are changing rapidly. Information takes on a different aspect as technology causes wider accessibility. As certain information becomes less scarce or less accurate, it becomes less valuable; therefore, its nature changes. For example, the layman can now freely access stock quotes from the world's largest markets via Internet, any time, any day. This means brokers no longer possess scarce information, but only the knowledge on how to use that information. The fact that an investor can now get this information in real time has lead to many people skipping the broker and attempt to manage and trade their own portfolios. As a result, brokers will have to develop a different information base in order to re-create any added value.

As information is continually in flux, its meaning, relevance and value are always evasive and can thus never be captured by a single phrase. Information is produced by and anchored and embedded within networks connecting signifiers and meaningful issues. These networks can be imagined as rich webs of meanings, dynamic inter-actions between multiple actors, where knowledge is created that only has a temporary meaning, and where those temporary mean-ings are collected. Hence, information is to be regarded as a dynam-ic process. As we showed earlier, turbulent interactions between dif-ferent stakeholders of a corporation prove that the complexity of business, organizational and management environments cannot be reflected by variables. The essence of complexity is defined by the lack of both linearity and fixed causalities.

The corporate world does not really speak about information in dy-namic terms. Consider, for instance, Human Resource Management Information Systems (HRIS). These are designed to help organize the many administrative and strategic variables for which the Hu-man Resources department is responsible. Starting from a given template of generic 'common best practices', information about payroll integration, world-wide tax administration, ex-patriate ad-ministration, tracking global assignments, recruiting employees, planning careers, monitoring health and safety, compensation and benefits, training and development: all of this is stored in pre-de-fined databases. This example shows the rather rigid and static ap-proach to information. Dynamism becomes possible by manually updating the databases, thus re-defining the links between different databases.

The impact of understanding information as a dynamic process can be illustrated by two examples. The first one is Christodoulou's de-scription of a simulation, where variable structures are used to han-dle complex situations.

Dynamic simulations are increasingly used as a strategy exploration tool, as they address the shortcomings of static analyses that most established frameworks offer. The following table summarizes and compares some of the widely used strategic analysis frameworks. These are all static in nature.

	Five Forces	*Core Competency*	*Game Theory*
Assumptions	Stable industrial structure	Firm as a collection of competencies	Industry as a dynamic oligarchy
Goal	Defence position	Sustained advantage	Temporary advantage
Performance	Industrial	Unique firm	Right 'strategies'
Driver	structure	competencies	(moves)
Strategy	Pick an industry, a strategic position, fit organisation	Create a vision, build and exploit competencies	Make the right competitive and co-operative moves
Success	Profits	Long-term dominance	Short-term gain

The most widely used framework for modeling and analyzing competitive industry dynamics is Porter's Five Forces model. The structure-conduct-performance paradigm upon which Porter's five forces are based, assumes that each player adopts a single, well-defined and unchanging role. In addition, it assumes that industry structure is fixed, only considering differences in average industrial profitability without taking into account rivals' choices as to whether to compete or not. Game theory models strategic decisions and offers valuable insight into matters of competition and negotiation, but looks at dynamic situations by means of a set of static equilibria. In addition, game theory assumes optimal behavior and perfect rationality on the part of the players.

Actual human decision-making, however, is often far from optimal and rational. Given the highly dynamic markets that firms operate on today, the problem we are faced with is how to model and simulate markets and economic systems that exhibit a similar complex behavior. The aim is to create a model for the development of the market and its participants over time, to gain a deeper understanding of how market works and finally to learn the best way to manage change.

Forrester's System Dynamics (SD) and Ninios' OO/DEVS are two of the more traditional platforms used for strategic business simulations. Their focus is primarily on the dynamic behavior that results from a given market structure. Once the structure and policy rules have been defined, the model will describe the dynamic behavior of the system, but system components and relations among components do not vary. The model might accurately capture the structure of a complex system, but this will only be valid for as long as the current taxonomy holds and remains unchanged. In other words, fixed structure models cannot anticipate and cannot account for changes that might occur in the composition of the system, leading to incorrect causal relations and models that need to be reformulated.

Simulations based on theories of artificial life, as were also described in a previous section, embrace the idea that aggregate (macro)-behavior cannot be thought of as the simple sum of behaviors of 'average' individuals. In addition, the taxonomy of the system studied does not necessarily remain fixed, but should be able to evolve over time. The complex systems one should be studying can be defined as a set of simple, heterogeneous, interacting agents capable of exchanging information with their environment, and capable of adapting their internal structure as a consequence of this interaction. The behavior of the (economic) agents at micro level could bring changes at the aggregate market level. More importantly, new agents can, when appropriate, enter the market.

The motivation for this approach is the need to model industries and markets that can endogenously change their own structure. This is achieved by treating individual players as agents and providing the means for entrance and exit of economic agents in a system (say, a marketplace), as well as for an exchange of information among them. Our concern is not with the situations that will finally emerge, but rather to describe the original system, to ascertain how agents act and react to circumstances and thus to understand the actual process of market evolution and the role that economic agents play in defining these changing structures. Our aim is to explore industries and markets with a multiplicity of actors that individually make assumptions about what will happen in the market and, as a result, bring about changes both at the individual (firm) and at the aggregate (market) level of observation. Hence, an economic organization should be seen as a dynamic, adaptive process of interactions among individuals ('agents') in realistic and complex environments. This type of model offers a useful way of looking at how market structures and organisations emerge.

The above demonstrates the 'structural limitations' of traditional modeling and simulation techniques and explores the changing industrial structures that can be the result of economic agents' behavior. This is shown in the figure below, where it is attempted to close the gap caused by a static approach in business simulations by moving from dynamic behavior to dynamic structure.

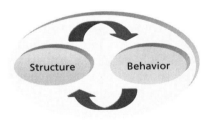

Figure 2.3 From dynamic behavior to dynamic structure

In doing so, it is possible to understand market dynamics at the level of the entire population by considering the actions and interactions of individual agents. One can also look at dynamic models of endogenous mergers and acquisitions, investment, entry and exit, using descriptive models based on decentralized agents whose collective interactions produce emergent behavior.

This approach perfectly fits the complexity theory, where the initial conditions of a system combined with the dynamic development path form a system. From an IT point of view, we propose an object-oriented framework that allows for changing model structure. This allows a model to dynamically adapt its structure during a simulation run. Economic agents are objects (in object-oriented programming terms) that interact with other agents through a series of messages. Each of them has a series of attributes and procedural methods with which it accomplishes things. The agents of the system do not simply react to external messages and data, but given the 'knowledge' they have, they can act as evolving, interrelated entities that have the ability to change their own environment.

This approach creates a tool for building models that can dynamically change their structure and can thus be used to study a range of interesting managerial problems. This methodology can therefore be used as a learning tool, where management teams can model and test their assumptions and explore future options. It is not intended to provide precise forecasts or make any statements about different outcomes.

Our second example, using Artificial Neural Networks (also described in a previous section) for building complex adaptive systems, carries the same idea a step further. In the first place, neural networks are 'trained' via a number of experiences. The neural network (which is a piece of software) attempts to learn patterns in such a way that it can reproduce all the cases it has learnt. Once a neural network has learned to reproduce cases, it can also produce new cases.

Neural networks show a remarkable capacity to 'learn' constantly. They learn from each new experience. The building of the information system never stops. Such systems can guide people through an information base, or through a learning environment, based on their preferences, pre-knowledge, experience, etcetera. The changing personal development path automatically offers the employee customized learning material for the career move that is being planned, or provides the corporate applications on the theoretical course followed the previous week. An evaluation system connected to such a learning environment feeds back into the personal development path, and in continuous interaction, dynamically adapts both the personal development path and the individualized learning environment. At a later stage, when we will look more deeply into the link between virtual learning and knowledge management (which we will call the Hybrid Business School), these links will prove to be of added value.

The same perspective is used in building knowledge-based approaches for identifying client profiles. One can construct a particular information system which is bound to just partly describe reality. It generates client profiles at a particular moment, for a particular market. The process of using the information systems continuously for both existing and new clients and markets creates new information that in turn allows the information system to 'learn' and adapt. Such complex adaptive systems show the desirable dynamic behavior, but another perspective on information systems is needed as well. The concept of the Hybrid Business School, as it will be developed in this book, fits this focus of information as a dynamic process, where the learner creates as much as he or she consumes.

2-3 Knowledge and Learning

Knowledge and Experience

In the cognitive sciences, and especially in epistemology, a great deal of research has been done in an attempt to identify and define knowledge. Unfortunately, we do not know what managerial knowledge really is. Even though we have vaguely understand, there are few definitions of knowledge within a 'managerial' context.

Kim (1993) suggested that knowledge is a combination of 'know-how' and 'know-why'. Other authors, including Nonaka, identify different types of knowledge, i.e., tacit and explicit knowledge. Explicit knowledge refers to formal, systematic language, the rules and procedures followed by an organization. This kind of knowledge is transferable, be it by means of education or by socialization. Knowledge-based systems are based on explicit knowledge. Tacit knowledge, on the other hand, is mainly based on lived experiences and therefore difficult to identify and transfer. Deeply rooted in action, commitment and involvement in a specific context, it refers to cognitive and technical qualities that are inherent to the individual.

Experience is a key factor in acquiring tacit knowledge. An example of tacit knowledge in business would be the decision-making process of financial markets dealers. Based on what they have learned from their past experiences, on what they read and hear, and on the 'climate on the market', brokers make buying and selling decisions within a split second. We like to call this 'gut instinct' or 'Fingerspitzengefühl', but the behavior of each dealer is different. They each seem to have their own way of dealing, based on experience and framework of reference. It has proven extremely difficult to extract this kind of 'knowledge' from dealers – not because they do not want to share it, but because it seems extremely difficult for them to express their knowledge, or in technical terms, to make tacit knowledge explicit. However, since some dealers are consistently better than others, it would be of interest to understand why they excel, e.g., in order to describe the principles of 'winning' behavior. Furthermore, if a dealer acquires his knowledge while working for a particular bank, how can this bank keep the acquired knowledge (asset), if this dealer leaves the company?

Many different types of cognitive elements are involved. Those that are of interest for managerial problems center on 'mental models' in which people form working models of the world by creating and adapting mental analogies. Mental models could be described as deeply held convictions of how the world works. They represent a person's view of the world, including explicit and implicit understanding. Mental models provide the context in which to view and interpret new material; they determine whether stored information is relevant to a given situation. There is a clear analogy between how mental models function and the way in which the human brain works. The human brain is characterized by a high degree of parallelism. This means that a large number of elements (in this case neurons) are used at the same time, alongside of each other. A second important characteristic of the human brain is the micro-structure of cognition (distributed knowledge) on which it is built. The human brain has no clear answer for what will happen in a given situation, but is able to construct solutions and actions quickly and easily, based on this micro structure of knowledge. Consequently, we can assume that knowledge is not sequential but parallel, and deals with variety – not with averages.

Based on these definitions of and analogies to individual learning, organizational learning is defined as increasing an organization's capacity to take effective action. The emphasis does not lie on reality but rather on perceptions of reality (meanings). It is clear from this description how crucial context is for learning and knowledge.

An organization's ability to take effective action is based on tacit corporate knowledge. The greater the accessibility of this corporate knowledge (but not necessarily the explicitness), the easier it is to use it. In management, perceptions of reality become more important than reality. Hence, the role of corporate mental models becomes increasingly important, since their ultimate aim is to visualize the shared mental model for any chosen subject. A shared mental model is fundamental to corporate learning, and hence to pro-active management. If we want to take this reasoning one step further, one could even consider the manager's role to be to identify the shared elements or unity within diversity (complexity). This idea introduces management of corporate (tacit) knowledge as a strategic mission.

From this idea of unity within diversity also follows that organizations are most creative when they operate away from equilibrium, in an area of 'creative tension'. This means thinking about the fractal nature of organizational boundaries and the realization that all employees are near to different boundaries of their organizations, and therefore understand only part of their firm's environment. Instead of absorbing complexity, diversity and, consequently, uncertainty, this idea has a richness to it, as it embraces development and creativity. According to Nonaka, such 'creative chaos' may need to be intentionally created by management throughout an organization, allowing for self-organization processes. If at this point, managers are not allowed time for reflection, creative chaos can become 'destructive chaos'. As a consequence, time should be built into managerial structures and processes.

Despite the variety of definitions, the organizational capacity for knowledge creation is gaining in popularity in managerial science. Some consider it to be a potential source of competitive advantage for companies. The organizational ability to translate all this information and knowledge into 'intelligence', i.e., to understand, connect, an exploit those resources in a distinctly competitive way, is crucial, however. Whereas companies have long been dominated by a paradigm that conceptualized the organization as a system that 'processes' information and/or 'solves' problems, nowadays, an organization is viewed as a knowledge-creating system. Its dynamic nature, continuous change, and discontinuous leaps that are part of such a system are essential. In order to describe a company's pool of knowledge, some authors use the metaphor of a 'cognitive map'. A cognitive map is a written plan in which a person expresses, using blocks and connecting arrows, how he or she reasons and how they connect things. In a similar vein, the term 'corporate IQ' is sometimes used, while others argue for a more quantitative representation of this body of knowledge and call it a 'fusion map'. These are all different ways of describing the same thing: a repository of (tacit and explicit) knowledge.

Learning and Mental Models

Learning could then be considered as progress. It represents an opportunity for individuals to pause, reflect upon and reframe issues and experiences not based on their own insights, but also on the interaction with others. Hence, learning is not abstract but contextual: it occurs at appropriate moments, in an appropriate quantity while the actual experience is taking place, so that it can be applied immediately. As such, learning can be seen as the process whereby knowledge is created by the transformation of experience. This definition of learning relates to Kim's 'know-how' and 'know-why'. According to this definition, learning takes place in a cycle of four steps. First, something is experienced within a particular context. Second, based on this experience, observations and reflections are generated. Third, based on these reflections, abstract concepts and generalizations are formed and fourth, these new ideas are tested which in turn results in new experiences. Again, these new experiences can become the first step in a new loop.

The idea of a cyclical learning loop is described in the so-called OADI-cycle (Observe – Assess – Design – Implement).

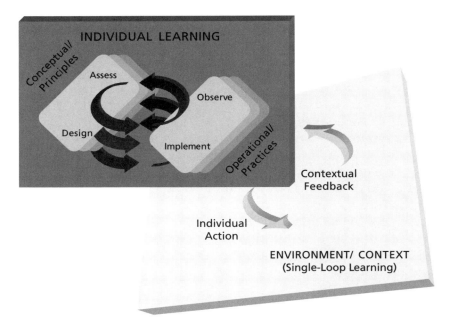

Figure 2.4 Simple model of individual learning – the OADI-cycle

An obvious example of this learning process is to observe how a child learns not to touch a hot stove. In many cases, a child cannot be taught not to touch a warm plate. The first time (even when told not to) a child attempts to touch a hot stove, it observes something that he assesses as heat. It decides, not necessarily consciously, on an action, probably to take away its hand. Eventually, the child implements that design and does take away its hand. A new observation follows which is assessed as being 'better'. At this point, no further decision takes place. In case the hand has already been burned, the child again observes something that is registered as unpleasant. It would (or in the beginning someone else would) assess it as 'burned'. A possible design would be to put his hand under cold running water, which he eventually does. This cycle can continue for a number of rounds. Via this process of 'learning the hard way', an individual, independent of age, learns by experience. Learning is inseparable from taking action and applying knowledge to events. The nature of that knowledge includes explicit as well as implicit understanding and meaning that the individual ascribes to events and their purposes. The single-loop process is implemented by individual action, which in turn creates a contextual feedback. Instruction can shorten the learning cycle, but only if the person in question understands. This means that the instruction should fit into this person's existing reference frame. As a result, instruction without embedding – contextualization – has little added value.

A second stage of individual learning, then, links individual learning with individual mental models. This process is called 'double-loop learning' as it is concerned with learning based on contextual impulses (as portrayed by the OADI-cycle) as well as learning from connecting the impulses of the individual's mental models.

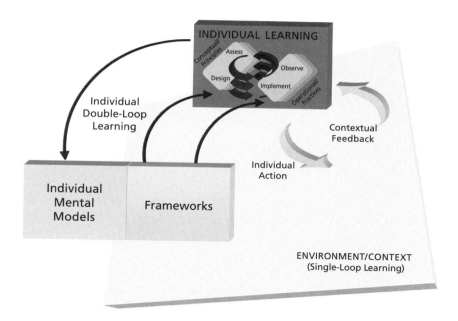

Figure 2.5 Double-loop individual learning

Let us take the example of the child again. When a child goes through the above-mentioned experience a number of times, it will not touch the stove again. The child does not necessarily know what is happening and it does not necessarily understand why a hot stove should not be touched. It has implicitly developed a framework of knowledge that allows it to deal with any similar cases, without knowing the correct equations. In some respects it can be argued that this is not a true example of learning, but rather of a human reflex. Probably this is true. However, it indicates clearly how the learning cycle operates in contextual interaction (single-loop learning) and how it leads to the individual mental model (via individual double-loop learning). According to the same principle, a commercial trader learns by doing and so creates his own mental model about trading. Any learning experience (courses, or books read) could speed up the process if, and only if, the experiences fit into the person's existing framework (mental model). If the gap between the existing mental model and the material taught is too large, little learning takes place. Teaching is no guarantee for learning: teaching is only one kind of experience that an individual can choose to use for learning purposes. Field experience can be another means for learning. Hence, different people react completely differently to the same learning experience. There is no single teaching method which is 'the' best, and no single way to learn which is 'the' best. Learning remains an individual act of free will.

We will now describe a comparable double-loop learning model on an organizational level. As is similar to the single-loop learning in the individual model, each individual action can be part of an organizational action, which in turn causes additional contextual feedback. This is called single-loop organizational learning. Double-loop organizational learning takes place when the individual mental models are grouped together to form shared mental models – shared on a corporate or group level – which in turn will influence the individual mental models. By means of exposing and questioning tacit knowledge it is possible, by a process of 'dialoguing', to create shared meanings, which create a sense of identity and purpose with which individuals in organizations can identify. In figure 2.6, shared mental models are also defined as organizational routines. It is especially these explicit shared models – the explicit organizational routines – that determine the learning ability of an organization.

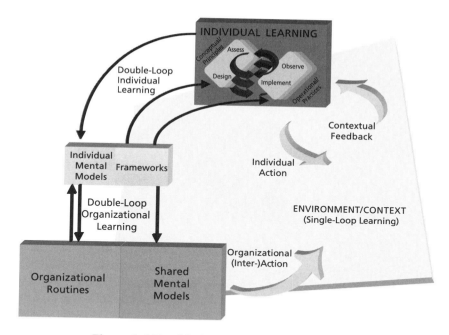

Figure 2.6 Double-loop organizational learning

Double-loop organizational learning can only take place by bringing together individual mental models in a learning space. Individual mental models are only created by individual learning experiences. One particular experience does not have a direct impact, neither on the individual mental models nor on the shared mental models. In other words, there exists no fixed causality between the two. Any change in the shared mental model happens individual experiences, which would first have to change the individual mental models before a learning experience could change a shared mental model. This does not mean that shared mental models are an addition to individual mental models, or that they are only the addition of a number of individual mental models. On the contrary, any attempt to change a shared mental model must be done through learning experiences at the individual level (even if these experiences take place in teams or groups). As an individual learns, changes may occur on the shared level, provided that the individual fits the new experience into his mental model. However, it remains almost impossible to foresee the impact on the shared model of an action on the individual level. A shared mental model, therefore, is not a static entity. It should be monitored constantly. This is what we understand by visualizing and comparing mental models.

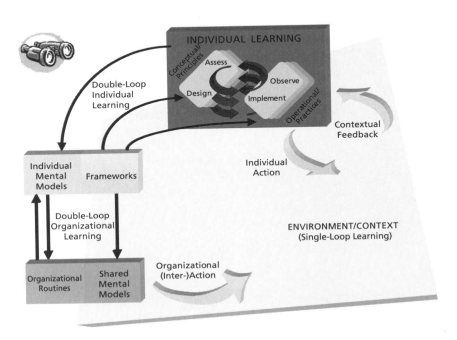

Figure 2.7 An integrated model of organizational learning

As such, knowledge management is an attempt to visualize mental models with the aim of learning from them and sharing them. As we have seen earlier, business is not only faster but also fundamentally different: it moves in a non-linear and unpredictable fashion. The crux lies in working out how all the forces and elements interact to shape an overall system and in determining its often surprising outcomes. As the flow of competitive events is discontinuous, and as it is impossible to predict the success of products or companies, it is obsolete to use analytical strategies, or to try to shape the organization to meet the needs of the business. Without an adequate base, knowledge management, and the organizational ability to absorb information, generate new ideas and put knowledge into practice, it is difficult for companies to keep on top of changing economic realities. Information is not just data, and knowledge not just its codification, but rather the ability to see patterns and to combine strategic resources, intellectual technologies, and processes, in order to understand, connect and exploit and knowledge in a uniquely competitive way. In short, organizations have to become learning organizations. To become a knowledge-creating and learning organization changes all of the assumptions underlying an organization's structures and processes, and will change the roles, responsibilities, skills and activities of all involved, especially those of managers. Organizational learning magnifies and closes the loop of individual learning within a dynamic corporate and networked setting, a company's learning process to exceed efficiency frontiers. Organizational learning will be spurred on by the organization's skills, which includes everything from resources, (infra-)structures and support systems to enabling constraints and core philosophy. Essentially, we are talking simple cognitive processes.

The best-known example of how a shared mental model differs from the simple equation of a number of individual mental models is undoubtedly the one of the caged monkeys and the bananas. This story is mainly used as a metaphor, and it is not argued here that monkeys have a mental model. If one puts 20 monkeys into a cage with a stepladder in the middle and a bunch of bananas on top, the smartest monkey runs up the steps and takes a banana. This monkey follows its 'individual mental model'. When the monkey takes the banana, it starts to rain. Monkeys do not like rain. Then, one monkey is taken out of the cage and replaced. The second smartest monkey runs up the step and, following its mental model, takes a banana. Again, it starts to rain. Allow us to draw your attention to the fact that each monkey is rained on, which gradually will influence its mental model. Again, a monkey is replaced. This story continues until the smart monkeys have understood the mechanism. Individually, they still like the bananas but they understand the consequences. The least intelligent monkey then tries to take a banana. That monkey has not yet understood the mechanism. Again it pours; again, a monkey is replaced. The new monkey will try and run up the stepladder. All the others, having understood, will not try anymore, but what is more, they will also try to stop the new monkey from taking a banana. The new monkey does not understand, but he cannot get to the banana. He follows the shared behavior without understanding. Another 20 replacements will be delivered to the cage full of monkeys that each would like to take a banana. As a group, they do not do so, but none of them knows why. The shared mental model clearly differs from the individual mental models. The change has taken place via constant observations and experiences of each individual monkey. None of them has had the same number of experiences, since they entered the cage at different times.

This story illustrates the learning process and also shows that a shared mental model can be completely different from the sum of the individual mental models. Change in a shared mental model only occurs via experiences on an individual level. The individual mental model will then influence the shared mental model. This happens all the time in a corporate environment. 'Why do we do it this way?' 'It's the way we've always done it.' Nobody necessarily knows why, and it is likely that the individual models will differ from the shared one. Is this what we call 'corporate culture'?

If we would like to alter a corporate culture, we cannot dictate the process of change: after all, it is non-linear and emergent. Steps will have to be undertaken so that each individual employee will have new experiences. If these new experiences are received in a positive atmosphere, individuals may – but cannot be forced to – integrate these new positive experiences into their individual mental models, which in turn, eventually, could change the shared model (i.e., corporate culture). It is a lengthy process, which is triggered by individual learning.

Management education is an important vehicle in developing 'emergent' strategies, knowledge management and the organizational skills that promote organizational learning. It can help in creating the right conditions for reflective thinking and learning. Referring to figure 2.7, management education could be seen as single loop learning. As the figure shows, environment/context (for instance, a business school) may play an important part by providing input for the learning process of individuals and groups. However, learning takes place in the double-loop areas; if it would not, the input of management education would be a waste of effort.

It is crucial, therefore, that management education and knowledge management are harmonized. They reinforce each other. Due to the existence of information technology, they can be easily integrated, which will result in a virtual business school. Technology, however, is only a means to an end. A context to the corporate learning and knowledge process should be provided that includes a certain pedagogical approach. A virtual business school needs all of these ingredients in order to be successful. First, a specific pedagogical approach and an appropriate mix of management education and knowledge management are crucial. Further, the business school must be able to offer specific knowledge and have a unique approach to learning, and must have a strong commitment to linking management education with knowledge management. Learning and knowledge processes are not static, as they rely on information, which is a dynamic process, as well as on human interactions. Finally, appropriate information technology should be used in order to support and reinforce educational activities, the knowledge factor, and communication.

After this extensive introduction to knowledge and learning, we will now position the role of virtual education. From a corporate point of view, management education comes into the picture with the single-loop learning, but only to the extent that it fits into the corporate knowledge approach. Management education, and particularly the use of IT in management education, creates added value if it can be joined with the corporate effort to manage knowledge. Management education can introduce concepts, cases, and activities, but it becomes even more interesting if, via a knowledge approach or network, these are taken a step further into a double-loop learning process

Based on IT, the virtual business school is the perfect environment for single-loop learning, transfer of contextual knowledge and creation of contextual input for learning. Management education should be a stimulus for further in-company learning as well as (shared) mental model building. Provided there is close cooperation with companies, business schools can play an important role in this process. When companies set up their own 'corporate universities', it is because they are dissatisfied with courses taught by business institutes, that are too general, as well as with the way management education is not tailored to fit their internal efforts, or with the costs of existing courses. But if companies set up their own 'corporate university' in order to organize the transfer of external knowledge, they risk cloning their own knowledge system (provided they have one). Or, rather than to create a university, they risk creating a knowledge-sharing system.

The most likely development is that business schools will start providing knowledge to companies in a flexible, hybrid way, i.e., by using technology. Combined with the companies' own knowledge management effort, this is the virtual business school approach. Ideally, business schools and companies should cooperate in the implementation of the overall concept of virtual education and knowledge management. The more closely the basis of management education and the knowledge base of a company are linked, the more added value it will have for a company. Business schools must therefore organize their courses differently by feeding into knowledge networks. This will be discussed later.

As has already been argued in the introduction, university administrators and faculty staff will need to be flexible. This development will change the role of the university and its faculties; it could even affect its status. If knowledge-creating processes using management education are to be imbedded so that the overall complexity of companies and management can be managed more easily, a greater emphasis will have to be placed on mindsets, learning and knowledge, both in management education in companies. This fact will affect both a company's approach and its structure/architecture. In this sense, there is still a long way to go. Joint efforts and developments in artificial intelligence, the cognitive sciences, and modern human resources management (i.e., strategic versus administrative and operational) will enhance knowledge management in a business environment. Another result will be the further development of organizational learning. Above all, however, business schools and companies should start cooperating on the implementation and deployment of integrated knowledge networks and learning platforms.

2-4 Building Stones for the Hybrid Business School

- Information is a dynamic process. Knowledge is concerned with the way one learns to fix the flow of the world in temporal and spatial terms.
- Business, markets, and organizations change in a discontinuous, non-linear and dynamic way, allowing for the possibility of emergent and self-organizing behavior. Emergence cannot be predicted or even envisaged from the knowledge of the behavior of each component of a system.
- No single concept of management captures the diversity of roles and activities in which managers are involved.
- The capacity of an organization to take effective action is based on tacit corporate knowledge. Knowledge management attempts to make explicit this tacit knowledge in order to learn from it and share it.
- Managerial competencies reflect the particularities of managerial roles. Managerial competencies are sustained by continuous learning.

References

- Baets, W. (1998). *Organizational Learning and Knowledge Technologies in a Dynamic Environment*. Kluwer Academic Publishers.
- Collins, J. & Porras, J. (1996). *Building your Company's Vision. Harvard Business Review*, September-October, pp. 65-77.
- Christodoulou, K. (1999). *Modeling and Simulation of Variable Structure Systems: A Way to Handle Complexity*, in: Baets, W. (Ed.), *A Collection of Essays on Complexity and Management*. World Scientific.
- Economist Intelligence Unit (1997). *Vision 2010. Designing Tomorrow's Organization*. London: The Economist Intelligence Unit.
- Kim, D. (1993). *The Link between Individual and Organizational Learning. Sloan Management Review*. Fall 1993.
- Nonaka, I. (1994). *A Dynamic Theory of Organizational Knowledge Creation. Organization Science*. Vol. 5, nr. 1.
- Pirsig, R. (1974). *Zen and the Art of Motor Cycle Maintenance*. Penguin.
- Prahalad, C. K. & Hamel, G. (1990). *The Core Competence of the Corporation. Harvard Business Review*. 68, nr. 3, pp. 79-91.
- Woodruffe, C. (1991). *Competent by any other Name. Personnel Management*, September, pp. 30-33.

Chapter 3

Business Education Environment

As we established in the previous chapters, managerial roles have changed and are still changing in nature. Logically, therefore, relevant managerial competencies must also change over time, and there is a justified need to discuss changing managerial competencies. Not surprisingly, managerial competencies, or the lack thereof, are the main focus for criticism from the companies as well as the business school community.

3-1 Criticisms from the Business World on Business Schools

The majority of criticism on business education stems from a lack of 'intelligence' in business and management graduates, which leads us to believe that the problem lies not in the curriculum per se, but rather in the educational approach. Some authors already have come to the conclusion that business education is not preparing students for the challenges of corporate life, as it is probably based on the wrong model of management education. These worries are also echoed in current literature. Research in the form of literature or executive interviews not surprisingly reveals several categories of criticism on management education. The following categorization will be generalizing, for the purpose of making a point. The first category is about 'too much'; the second about 'too little'.

A major point of criticism concerns too great a focus on the transfer of 'best past practices'. Given the particulars of each individual company and the turbulence and complexity in which they have to operate, education should focus on 'best principles' rather than 'best practices'. As every manager knows, blueprint answers to blueprint questions are rarely effective. Practices must be reduced to a more conceptual level of principles, in order to be able to study challenges and find answers. Principles can then be translated into a specific future context. It is in this ability of playing between levels that a manager's strength should lie.

Another important factor is that principles change over time. Principles are more easily adapted than practices, which are far more rigid. Working with principles also teaches participants to develop a conceptual insight, and a cohesive mindset about management, as well as a theory of practice, which will provide them with greater powers of strategic analysis. But how many students and course participants can really translate a managerial phenomenon into a concept, comprehend as a result of asking pertinent questions, and turn this comprehension into practice? Where is that critical distance?

There is also too much 'story telling' going on in business schools. Too much anecdotal information, lacking deeper conceptual ground or clear relevancy, is given. Graduates return to or arrive at their company with often heroic stories, without really knowing how these relate to a specific challenge they are facing. Connected with this, there is also too much emphasis on transferring knowledge rather than transferring learning. Acquiring knowledge is one thing, but learning to learn, whether it be as part of a continuous development or learning from a particular situation, is quite another. The ideal understanding of a career as a sequence of learning and development experiences is not really common in either MBA or MBA-type programs or in more traditional programs.

A large percentage of management programs are too functional and discipline-oriented. These are based on a view of management and business as a 'learned' profession. An important element of this 'professionalization' of business programs is their insistence on a division of subject matter into categories (functional areas or domains) that each have separate conceptual bases, as opposed to an interdisciplinary and multidisciplinary complexity with a common ground. Advocates of this 'professional approach' claim that one can only truly understand the overall picture and become more efficient in one's decision-making through compartmentalization.

In most business-type programs, however, it is up to the participants to put the pieces of the overall jigsaw into place, that is, to understand how the separate categories relate to a whole 'program'.

One wonders how many students actually manage to do so without proper guidance, i.e., can really understand management by compartmentalizing. Looking at MBA students who have to engage in a business simulation running a mock company, where they must take into account the dynamics between different functional areas and between economic agents: only a minority succeeds. As expected, most players focus on the different functional areas of the company one at a time, not going beyond the trivial and obvious. They practice analytic detachment over integrative insight, which proves that management is more than the sum of its components.

Like the functional and discipline-oriented approach, the rational quantitative approach (as opposed to the qualitative approach) is overly stressed in business programs. For example, when looking at management in terms of complexity and flux, a qualitative approach would have added value. The richness of managerial life and business cannot be solely translated in figures, but requires – as every manager knows – a qualitative approach. Even when dealing with figures, a qualitative assessment of these figures is needed. Qualitative methods such as mind-mapping and decision-making can offer an insight in how to manage complexity, rather than managing complexity – this is embedded in a purely quantitative approach. The manager, however, cannot control the increasing complexity of organizational life by using a template of pure functional rationality.

Executives also criticize business institutions for having too much of a focus on technical problem-solving in which problems are found, isolated, and then 'clinically' analyzed. This could be called the engineering or technocratic approach to management. Inherently, there's an overemphasis on cognitive learning which focuses on theories, models and facts. This approach gives students the impression that there has to be an answer – *the* answer – to every problem. In other words, management problems can be fitted into neat, narrowly specialized technical packages. As explained earlier, however, a manager's strength lies in asking pertinent questions, and in taking advantage of the richness of complexities and turbulence to guide him in his problem-solving. Because in real managerial life the 'and ... and' must prevail over the 'or ... or': the 'genius of the and' dominating the 'tyranny of the or'. There is no such thing as *the* answer, and it is too limiting to even think in those terms. Travelling between tensions or extremes ('and') and making use of those tensions and contradictions allows the search for openings that make new choices possible. It is one of today's managerial core competency boundaries.

We would like to start our second category of criticism – the 'too littles' – by pointing out a serious lack of cross-cultural awareness in most business programs. Cultural awareness and academically-based cross-cultural courses seem to receive little attention in most institutions and programs. A one-day seminar on cross-cultural management or working in groups with participants from different countries throughout the program is commonly thought to be enough to integrate cross-cultural skills. This is not the case, which hardly surprises when it transpires how few faculty members have truly international experience, have worked in different countries and experienced different management styles. To what extent are professors really of cultural bias and assumptions in management models, concepts, techniques or theories? Is it enough to explain this bias to students and participants? In short, a truly international scope is lacking in many programs.

Not only is there too little cross-cultural awareness embedded into programs, there is also too little future-orientation in many business programs. Often, out-dated models and theories are still being taught. Most of the strategic concepts that are still used, for example, were developed in the 1920s. New and innovative concepts based on new economies, a changing business world, modern organizational processes and the new roles of managers are rarely touched upon. For example, how many programs include seminars or courses on the application of complexity and chaos theory to change management, manufacturing or economy? The disadvantage of focusing on leading-edge ideas, however, is that the corporate world has yet to embrace them. At any rate, it is imperative to establish a balance and make students understand how to self-evolve and gradually implement new ideas and perspectives. Students have to be cleverly convinced of the need for a future-oriented mindset, and be taught not to fear punishment from the corporate world for being future-oriented. This brings us to the fact that too many programs foster risk-averse attitudes in their participants.

One of the criticisms mentioned earlier pertained to the fact that business programs do not facilitate the development of a conceptual and cohesive mindset regarding management, which would provide participants with greater powers of strategic analysis based on working with principles as opposed to practices. Individuals need to be able to reflect on managerial practices and develop an epistemology of inquiry that allows them to contribute to the knowledge base by being able to ask the pertinent questions. The habit of reflection would also help free managers from habitual and rigid ways of looking at phenomena, and to increase their alertness, creativity and innovative powers. In business education, however, insufficient attention has so far been paid to 'reflective management', and to steering the theory of practice. As a consequence, graduates have trouble developing vision, and in articulating and communicating that vision. Instead, they have a short-term rather than a long-term focus.

In addition, insufficient attention is given to processes. Working in teams is one thing, but understanding group dynamics and coaching, and being able to give and receive feedback is quite another. A common complaint is that the development of behavioral skills receives no priority in business education. Personal and personality development are elements most schools do not particularly focus on. It is assumed that these skills will develop automatically as a result of the pressures of an MBA-type program or intense management development seminars. This is a 'drifting' approach to learning which does not steer students towards the important points, leaving a very high margin for error. For instance, students could end up not understanding the importance of personal development, as well as not being able to help others develop. The lack of personal and personality development is also illustrated by the way students are assessed. Assessment should not only include academic but also managerial and organizational components and also incorporate a broader strategic perspective which focuses on the student's ability to grasp the complexities and turbulence of modern business, and of organizational and managerial environments. Moreover, business education needs to convey a philosophy of management development that is a continuing process of development and learning-to-learn.

It has been said that most business programs emphasize social capital (networking) under the umbrella of intellectual capital (knowledge), while completely ignoring cultural capital. Indeed, few institutions further the development of a mature view on geopolitics and socio-economic trends. Even fewer attempt to increase the overall cultural level of their customers, for example by promoting the development of esthetics, the art of living, or an appreciation of philosophical and cultural differences – all of these things actually create meaning in the world in which they work as media where the senses and wisdom meet.

An important number of educators and program coordinators will claim to have dealt with the criticisms the business community has identified. Indeed, there are programs that have incorporated part of these criticisms, and there are programs that are specifically aimed at dealing with these criticisms. Some institutions have responded by starting specialized courses or seminars, others have initiated a personal development track, and still others have tried integrative modules or 'learning-by-doing' projects (i.e. action-learning). An interesting point remains however, which is that the business community has been voicing its disappointment with the same areas of business teaching for at least the past 20 years. The question is, then, whether pedagogical models have actually fundamentally changed, or if indeed there is still a lot of critical work to do.

3-2 Pedagogical Metaphors

Pedagogical metaphors are used to describe a school's existing paradigms or approaches, and the role of its different players. A look at these metaphors will clarify the essence of some of the criticisms described earlier. We will synchronically present some of the established metaphors. Over the years, the transfer metaphor has been the prevailing one.

The transfer metaphor describes education as a theory of knowledge or subject matter that is considered a transferable commodity. The student is viewed as a (passive) vessel positioned alongside a loading dock, while the teacher is a crane or a forklift. The teacher delivers and places knowledge into the empty vessel until it is full. Once the vessel is filled, a 'bill of loading', which is the diploma, certifies the content of the vessel. Monitoring a student means monitoring the process of filling the vessel and sometimes sampling the quality of the contents. When students fail, teachers will say that the vessel is no good. At the same time, the student will blame the forklift. It is clear that programs which are based on the transfer theory are very much lecture-based, including lectures from leading figures in the relevant fields (the more the better), providing students with duplicate course notes. The 'in search of excellence' literature that was started by Peter and Waterman perfectly illustrates this metaphore. Conceptual routines are complemented by dynamic examples and prescriptions derived from the exploits of corporate heroes and 'excellent' companies. Combined with the professional orientation to management, this type of approach is still prevalent in most business schools.

The next metaphor is referred to as 'the shaping theory'. In this metaphor, the student enters school as a piece of inert raw material, like a piece of wood or metal. The teacher is the craftsman who is able to shape the material, using subject matters as tools. Teaching methods that apply to the shaping theory include workshops, practical instructions similar to recipes and exercises with predictable outcomes. Again, students are seen implicitly as passive learners in the sense that they cannot take charge of their own learning and that they cannot use conceptual knowledge unless re-interpreted for them and delivered using carefully reconstructed methods. Instructors go to great length to ensure a well-presented and fine-tuned delivery, and to make sessions active and practical using nicely sequenced hands-on activities, cases, and exercises. As a consequence, the monitoring process focuses on the size and shape of the wood or the metal as it is being worked. If it all goes wrong, the student will blame the teacher for being a bad craftsman (i.e. bad delivery), whereas the teacher will say that the raw material is of poor quality. Some of the educational reforms are based on this shaping theory. The shaping theory, in conjunction with the transfer theory, accounts for most business school curricula today.

The 'travelling metaphor' has quite a different approach. The teacher takes the role of the experienced and expert guide who initiates and guides the students through an unknown terrain that he or she needs to explore. The guide not only points out the way, but also provides navigation tools and techniques: maps and compasses. The most common 'teaching methods' (if one can still call them such) used with the travelling theory are experiential: simulations, projects, action-learning exercises with unpredictable outcomes, discussions and independent learning. Action-learning emphasizes learning-by-doing. It is based on the idea that students learn more effectively with and from managers and teachers while all are engaged in the solution of actual, real-time and real-life problems occurring in a work-setting, applying the normal business pressures and constraints of organizational realities to ensure a high-quality outcome. In programs that embrace this theory, monitoring means regularly comparing each other's travelling notes. Instructors blame student's failure on unwillingness to take risks, be creative, or to accomplish objectives. From the student's point of view, the teacher can be blamed for poor guidance, poor equipment, and imposing too many restrictions. Indeed, teachers that work within this approach must not only have mastered the use of specialized skills, equipment, and expertise, but also have to possess a good working knowledge of the 'terrain'. Organizational sponsors can hamper the process by sanctioning projects and, as a result, hamper active learning. Experiments have shown that this theory is particularly effective in postgraduate level education.

The 'growing theory' takes this one step further. In many respects, this metaphor does not differ greatly from the previous one. It is an extension of the travelling metaphor, focusing on students' own initiative. Rather than creating a body of knowledge, thus defining the managerial profession (as is the case with the professional approach), course subjects are seen as a set of experiences each student should absorb. Hence, the student's overall aim should be to focus on his or her personality. The student is pictured as a garden in which everything has already been planted, but still needs to grow. However, grass cannot be made to grow quicker by pulling it. The teacher's role is that of a gardener, i.e., a tutor, but he must be careful not to overwork the garden. Creating a lush green garden takes hard work and much nurturing, but too much water or too much pruning will have a negative result. Hence, the gardener has to delicately balance constraints and guidance. The methods used are very much the same to those used with the travelling theory, but the student is allowed even more freedom and room to experiment. Also, the teacher is not sole repository of knowledge. As it is assumed that in order to become a manager the student also needs to develop his own personality, the monitoring process monitors the student's personal development. An ideal learning environment is created if the student is committed and has realistic expectations and is coached by an expert in personal development.

3-3 Challenging Educational Principles

We have discussed some of the consequences of the rapid, discontinuous, and non-linear changes of today's economy, the resulting quantitative and qualitative leaps (flux), the technological revolution, the collapse of time and space, and the increasing complexity of so many aspects of corporate and managerial life. Another important issue is the way educational principles are challenged today. If education today should prepare students for highly dispersed, flexible, unstable organizations with great emphasis on value-reinventing processes, education should be concentrated on developing the ability to identify, understand and articulate information, experience and knowledge. Hence, the learning environment should seen as a place where students and professors can discover and develop their personal style, as well as their understandings and insights in an integrated way.

The major challenge, then, is to bring theory and practice together rather than have theory and practice develop separately. As has already become clear when discussing the criticisms, the point of theory should be to provide students with a framework with which to translate a phenomenon to a conceptual level, arrive at an understanding by asking pertinent questions, and to translate this understanding to a practical level. The practice offered in the framework of a traditional program, however, is seen as a supplement to lectures, and as such is separated from real practice. This constitutes a first challenge, namely: how to unify theory and practice?

Further, as we explained, management education is traditionally and mainly designed around different disciplines (marketing, finance, etcetera) that each have separate theories and different conceptual bases that presume to reflect the separate functions identified as constituting the field of management. This phenomenon is also known as compartmentalization. The different component parts are separately taught to students by focusing on input and on the right courses for the right disciplines. The challenge lies in bringing theory on the level of practice where it concerns teaching methods and the curriculum.

On Theory and Practice

What are theory and practice all about? Theories can be situated on the dividing line between epistemology and a philosophical psyche. They are networks of intelligibility, knowledge, experience and meanings occurring within a turbulent environment. It is important, however, to look beyond the content of knowledge and not treat it as merely an informational commodity, but to focus on its dynamic process as well. The educational community should take an interest in the potential of theories to create new possibilities. Theories offer practice with developing critical distance and a cohesive mindset. In other words, what is needed is the opportunity to think about matters as psychological events. Hence, educators should approach theories as 'reflection-in-action'. This 'reflection-in-action' gives rise to the development of an epistemology of inquiry, which allows students to contribute to the knowledge base by being able to ask pertinent questions. Concerned as it is with understanding the origin, nature and validity of knowledge, i.e., the theory of (in this case) inquiry, reflection-in-action includes an epistemology of practice. Hence, theory and practice become inseparable. In other words, the answer lies not in the business simulations, personal journals, peer reviews, specific team-building and leadership modules, multi-disciplinary case studies and computer simulations that are used to make business education more pragmatic. An epistemology of inquiry based on working with best principles will enable people to take a critical distance and to discover limitations. It offers an integrative insight and an ability to translate a managerial phenomenon to a conceptual level. Hence, the answer lies much more in an overall teaching philosophy to which the art of inquiry is central.

Teaching in a Learning Community

Teaching, as Lundberg suggested, is becoming less of a 'set of problems to be solved' than 'a set of dilemmas to live with'. New ways are needed to understand and manage the anxiety and confusion associated with complexity, paradoxical roles, constant innovation, identities and meanings that arise from the here-and-now. Answers to problems become problems about answers. Knowledge and information are concerned with learning to fix the flow of the world in temporal and spatial terms and create order in managerial complexity and chaos. This can be reflected in the learning environment by attaching value to a difference in perspective. Examining competing frames of reference will result in a plurality of discourses and mindsets, which is preferable to reducing student's perception to a single all-including grand 'master theory'. As could be seen earlier, theories provide the framework within which events can be analyzed in a psychological way. If a particular issue is looked at from different perspectives, theories and disciplines in order to identify the underlying principles and structuring processes, the result will be a greater body of knowledge. Diversity also makes clear that knowledge itself becomes a matter of governance.

In transferring knowledge, teachers are invited to act as mentors, facilitators and helpers that make tacit knowledge more explicit by means of a subtle mixture of coaching, negotiated authority and a certain measure of freedom. In this process, sometimes the teacher takes responsibility for learning, and sometimes the students do. Students work with their mentors and learn by a mix of observation and practice. The close working-relationship between them is the result of a mixture of education and knowledge creation, of dialogs that create shared meanings, of ethics and esthetics. Knowledge sometimes has to be re-packaged for students and delivered by carefully constructed methods and substantial debate. As such, coaching and 'learned' freedom create experiences that can be further developed and applied. It is in this way that an epistemology of inquiry can be developed. Hence, the educational setting should be configured as a collaborative forum, a learning community in which different stakeholders such as program heads, faculty staff, executives, advisory boards, corporate action-learning sponsors, and students are all engaged in developing comprehension, approaches and an unlimited number of different perspectives. Within this learning community, stakeholders are partners in a mutual undertaking which advances learning and in this way help shape education. The learning community acts as a vehicle for sharing experiences, information, ideas, and knowledge, for detecting of patterns, as well as combining resources and intellectual technologies. Members will also receive moral and emotional support. In other words, this learning community is really a learning organization.

Active participation should be seen as an opportunity to interpret the world from the student's point of view and frame of mind. By offering students a platform for free dialogue, individuals are confronted with challenges that are paradoxical and which cannot always be defined or resolved. At the same time the role of the learning community must be emphasized. Communities are a platform for individuality, participation, and differentiation. The 'open' learning environment in which different learning situations take place simultaneously, such as the diversity of working and content forms, perspectives, and issues, presents a major challenge.

It is clear that experience and knowledge creation are not just based on information-processing. Students are not simply passive recipients of knowledge but co-creators of their own'-and-now' learning. Learning is characterized by interpretation rather than by description and analysis. It is a journey through the real world and through networks of meanings that will lead to greater knowledge of self as well as self-development. This knowledge of self should also for instance concern preferred learning style(s).

An Integrated Curriculum

The discussion should now be taken one step further and move from teaching philosophy to program philosophy, i.e., to the curriculum. As was mentioned before, business schools and management institutes have been altering the design of their programs in response to different criticism pertaining to the model of business education. This model is based on technical proficiency similar to that required for solving straightforward problems in mathematics, physics, or engineering. The left-hand curve in figure 3.1 shows how this functional and compartmentalized approach has been part of business programs since the 1970s. Has the business curriculum changed at all since then?

Essentially, traditional changes have concerned more integrative clusters that weave together common themes from multidisciplinary angles, action-learning-based consulting projects, or personal development tracks. These have been included in some management education programs since the second half of the eighties, but mostly only since the nineties. This is shown in the right-hand curve.

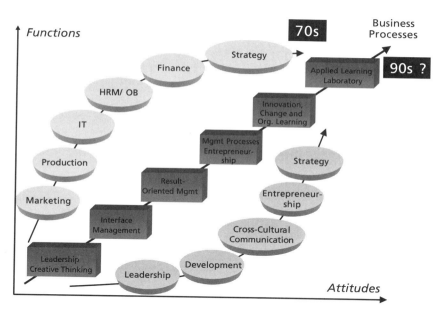

Figure 3.1 The integrated curriculum

Many institutions use a mixture of the two approaches: starting with some functional courses, programs will move on to focus on more integrative modules. A common alternative uses integrative modules to conclude every semester or block of functional courses. At the very least, this should help students to integrate insights and to create a better understanding of how the different classes relate to the program as a whole. Although in most cases the student is still considered to be a passive learner, aspects of the travelling metaphor can be found in programs that are combined with an experiential approach.

Some institutions take this a step further and offer programs that have a common theme. By this, we do not mean the 'major' that is offered by some MBA programs, but a complete MBA program. This can have a common theme such as technology, or luxury brand management. Moreover, in corporate (executive) education, few programs really have a well-defined theme that underlies and determines the whole program. This theme should truly reflect the philosophy and design of that particular program.

Others offer programs that are completely problem- or issue-based. Managerial roles, however, are seldom about just solving problems – whether they are straightforward or not. Moreover, problems are not central to managerial roles, since not everything a manager is presented with is a problem. Again, this is reflected by the technocratic or professional approach whose starting-point is the assumption that through problem-finding and problem-solving, stability, coordination, integration, and the implementation of functionality are pursued.

In a recent report, the Economist's Intelligence Unit stated that the key factor for driving an organization's competitive advantage, is a focus on business processes. This is consistent with the more recent management paradigms that increasingly appreciating business, organizational and strategic processes as the focal point for value creation and value reinvention. Also, the new economic realities and their complexities as described in the beginning of this book illustrate the importance of understanding processes.

We are convinced that the future of 'the' business school will entail curricula focusing on business processes, progressing towards the use of a learning laboratory. The third arrow in figure 3.1 illustrates this perspective. Mental models are also central to the design of learning laboratories. Laboratories are mental model practice grounds, where people develop the skills to have a dialogue about their assumptions in 'real time' – i.e., at the very moment they are dealing with an issue. This practice ground teaches people to talk coherently about beliefs and attitudes, to hear others' views on them, to question them, and to look at sources and opportunities.

3-4 Experiences with Educational Technologies in Management Development: Lessons for the Future

For companies, the surge in management development initiatives and increasing executive education is not just about gaining an edge in the market. Along with a vibrant economy, companies are using it as a way of fostering or winning back the loyalty of the troops, re-capturing lost talents, or luring new employees. Recent mergers, joint ventures and alliances have enhanced the role of corporate education and corporate universities. The growing demand, however, goes hand in hand with rising standards. Flexibility, customized and real-time programs, as well as efficient use of time both inside and outside the office: these are some of the new main focal points. In the next part, we will demonstrate how these demands have resulted in the rise of new educational technologies. What lessons can be learned from the various players in the educational arena?

'Open Learning' Experiences

In most countries, the academic institutes created in order to experiment with open or distance-learning are called Open Universities (OUs). The call for these Open Universities was a result of the movement towards lower entrance barriers for university degrees in the 60s and 70s. Furthermore, authors and philosophers such as Ivan Illich advocated continuous, life-long learning. Open Universities were not created to cater for the same groups as regular universities but rather to the 'convenience' and 'second chance' markets. As a result, OUs developed greater experience with more flexible forms of management education. Because of this experience in creating a more 'open learning' environment (long-distance learning), OUs come closest to having what is called a 'virtual' approach. As such, Open Universities are now becoming part of the 'virtualization race'.

The virtual business school, or a virtual approach to education, is commonly understood to mean the use of information technology, and increasingly, network technology is replacing the classical educational model of classroom instruction. Students receive course material electronically via Internet, or on CD-ROMs, and they use networks in order to communicate with their tutors or fellow students. Some forms of virtual education use a synchronous mode: teacher and student can communicate in real-time, as for example with video-conferencing. Other forms use the a-synchronous mode, where the student can use the network for various purposes, for instance e-mail, but does not have two-way on-line communication. Most web-based teaching is a-synchronous. What is commonly known today as virtual education is an IT-based replacement of the pedagogical transfer mode that is used in classical classroom teaching.

The transfer paradigm, however 'open', flexible and tailor-made, is still prevalent within the Open University environment. Generally speaking, the approach is rather traditional. Students are given paper-based and electronic material, and they are in touch with tutors by means of regional centers or a main campus. The material generally focuses on questions of reflection and individual activities. These activities, however, do not necessarily help develop management skills. Group activities are limited or non-existing, and there is not a great deal of project-based work. In the end, assuming that knowledge can be transferred and measured, exams decide who will be awarded a degree. Particularly in the case of management education and practicing managers, the measurement of knowledge as a single yardstick for learning is, as was argued before, questionable.

The flexibility offered by Open Universities is shown by the distance-learning as well as the flexible time aspects. Every student can deal with the material at his or her own pace depending on available time. There is little or no flexibility, however, in the courses or the different degree programs on offer. It should be recognized, though, that distance-learning material created and developed by Open Universities is generally of good educational quality and design.

The need for continuous and flexible learning is increasing, and as distance-learning is deemed to be a lucrative business, several regular universities and institutes jumped on the bandwagon. For example, Europe's Henley Management School has entered the Open University market by offering flexible distance-learning programs and by establishing small campuses in Europe and the Commonwealth. Likewise, the US-based University of Phoenix was a pioneer in distance-learning and now boasts thousands of degree students, using a mixture of on-line electronic and classical methods. Other technology used consists of audio and video tapes as well as video conferencing.

Duke's Fuqua School of Business is one of the first to offer a first-class electronic MBA program by using a platform of leading-edge applications. Students have CD-ROM video lectures in which the professor appears to be teaching live on screen, and they have supplement video and audio-programs which can be downloaded. Further, they work with peers via bulletin boards, e-mail and live chats. Finally, there is also still face-to-face contact with members and fellow students. Some two-week mandatory modules for on-site classes and meetings with business owners from Europe, China, South America and the United States are part of the program.

Over the last decade, we have seen a rapid move of many 'classical' universities, including the top US programs such as Stanford and MIT, into the same market of distance-learning based on IT. These universities concentrate their effort on regular students, rather than on the 'second chance' student of Open Universities. The vast number of universities offering 'on-line education' today proves there is a growing interest in the use of IT in management education.

Despite the vast amount of open learning that is being offered by regular universities, as well as the acquired experience, the paradigm of the educational process has not yet changed. Open learning still happens to be based on the transfer paradigm, in which IT is viewed as the crane that loads the empty ship quickest. The more regular universities enter into the market of open learning, the greater will be the focus on content and 'brand' of a degree. The Open Universities, at least, focused on the pedagogical side of the educational process right from the start.

Conferences about on-line education focus on the experiences of distance-learning in both Open Universities and regular universities offering distance-learning. By looking at different experiences in distance-learning environment, both from the point of view of OUs and regular universities we can investigate what lessons could be learned and applied to future developments.

We shall commence with the experience of OUs, as they have made a major contribution to the existing knowledge of IT and education. The working definition here of Open Universities is that of a kind of mega-university with a student population of over 100,000. OUs are growing rapidly due to the world-wide and ever increasing need for education, particularly in the third world. As the volume of potential students increases, IT-based distance education becomes a more efficient and less expensive way to learn. Broadband PC connections, however, are not yet widely available, so large-scale technological usage in OUs cannot be implemented. As a consequence, these mega-universities use the same technology and methods as do regular universities. Open Universities, for example, use a great deal of audio and video tapes and (public) broadcasting.

The British OU is a good example of this approach. Today, Open Universities experiment with 'personal casting', which entails transmitting programs via the net onto the student's PC. This remains a one-way method, however. Open Universities experiment also with remote classrooms, particularly in countries like Australia, where distance is the main reason for their success.

Increasingly, those running Open Universities are discovering the 'knowledge media' that support conversational paradigms and community ideas. Particularly within this evolution towards knowledge media, the sheer number of students they target become a burden regarding the IT development they would like to undertake. Students experiment with e-mail, a-synchronous computer conferencing (comparable to chatting over the Internet), Internet/www and stand-alone multimedia, but due to the large numbers of students, the interaction remains limited. OUs teach us that IT is indeed able to improve the value of learning, but so far, IT cannot cater to large numbers.

In experiments by regular universities, web-based teaching is often used in conjunction with distance-learning. Course material is presented on the Internet, as well as via electronic conferencing (mostly a-synchronous). Tutors support students via e-mail. In this way, students can create their own agenda. There is also an attempt to foster electronic teamwork amongst students, but with varying degrees of success. Regular universities do succeed in using multi-media (including video) to make case-studies more attractive, and for language learning.

There are also lessons to be learned from the experiences of universities in distance-learning. Recent conferences such as the IFIP conference on Virtual Education and the Educa On-Line Conference highlighted a few interesting points.

The first challenge is the need for accreditation, and in general, more status for open learning degrees. Traditionally, a university's credibility stems from its physical existence and its 'knowledge resources', including faculty and the tradition of the university. IT-based approaches basically lack these physical assets, causing confusion firstly about credibility, especially if obtaining a degree remains the main purpose of the OU-student. It is fair to say that among academics, open learning is not considered to be of the highest standards. As we will point out later in this chapter, this lack of credibility may be one of the reasons why corporate (virtual) universities have become more popular. The accreditation and credibility within a corporate environment is given by the employer, which is at least clear and direct; there are concise purposes and consequences.

A second challenge that needs to be met in order for IT-based distance-learning to become successful is the creation of digital libraries, which will help a purely web-based approach to succeed. The web-based teaching approach offers a wide range of otherwise scarce resources via the Internet, but it generally lacks books and articles, important sources for learning.

As was previously briefly stated, companies are increasingly entering the market of flexible learning. The corporate presence in flexible learning has evoked some interesting debate concerning the open-learning courses on offer at regular universities. The web is central to most corporate and academic educational experiments. Often, companies start by offering part of the educational process themselves, but companies organize the learning process differently. Corporate learning tends to be learner-centered, but relatively weak in the content part of the courses. Universities, however, remain organized in functional areas, so any distance-learning courses they offer follow this functional subdivision. The knowledge content of individual courses is therefore stronger, but the overall programs often lack integration and a clear focus on managerial competencies. Within a corporate setting, education is much more skill-based and problem solving-oriented.

Based on these experiences, there are other observations we can make. For example, the more IT is used in education, the more intense communication becomes; therefore in order to remain manageable, smaller the group of students who work together should be. Also, we can question whether the transfer paradigm can be continued to be used when the aim is individualized management education of experienced people.

The experiments that both universities and companies are involved in raise the fundamental issue: are we witnessing a technological evolution or a fundamental paradigm shift? The observation that it appears to be harder to introduce IT-based education in existing university settings than in corporate settings, seems to suggest it concerns a paradigm shift. The fundamental paradigm shift we propose is that management education should become more learner-centered, with the long-term perspective being to create individualized management education: just-in-time, just enough, and 'just right' education.

Corporate virtual universities are rapidly becoming popular, and therefore we would now like to touch upon corporate experiences in management education. Firstly, we will describe experiences with corporate management development programs; secondly, we will relate that experience to the role of IT in corporate management education.

The Corporate Educational Environment

Although business schools and management institutes control the bulk of the management development market, some newer approaches have recently been popping up in companies' in-house programs, corporate knowledge institutes or corporate universities. Potentially, the most appropriate corporate education will help develop the skills and competencies individuals are lacking and those which a particular company needs, to be incorporated into a company-wide organizational development project, in which the core values and culture of the learning organization can be established. In a Business Week report on executive education, it is said there are to be about 1,200 corporate universities in the United States. This number is growing rapidly, a trend that is also catching on in Europe. Some of the techniques used in these innovative programs are a clear (and sometimes complete) focus on the company's issues and bottom-line goals, action-learning inside projects, mentor programs, and self-teaching and learning in a group. Business school staff and experts in the field have a variety of roles in these programs such as those of internal consultants, teachers, project-supervisors, program designers, liaison between the company and the providers, and program coordinators. Together with faculty members, company leaders and speakers run sessions and deal with real-life business cases. This trend not only enhances content and delivery, but many companies find it is an aid in career development and an excellent development strategy to bring about strategic change and organizational growth processes. Also, the costs are lower. Specific modules from one program, for example, can be re-designed and used in another training and development path. Finally, it is more flexible. As there is no single business school that is strong in every field, it enables companies to look for the individual professors and experts that suit the company's needs or industry, and work directly with them. This explains why some of the more innovative programs are found not in business schools, but within the corporate institute environment.

The Case of a Corporate MBA

One innovative example can be drawn from the European headquarters of a high-tech multinational that developed plans for its own European corporate MBA program, based on a consortium model. The company has been confronted with strong competition, changing technologies, changing customer demands and changing market segments. The less loyal customer started to demand more sophisticated and reliable products and better service. As a consequence, the company designed a new vision for the future, taking into account the changing markets and business infrastructures. The new competitive agenda included new objectives and goals based on the development of core competencies and an increase in necessary skills, an improvement in the innovation process, as well as in the distribution of knowledge, entrepreneurship, and creativity. The project commenced with an assessment of the firm's human capital as well as its needs for the future. This assessment provided the basis for the general management development plan. Cultural change was to individual development. Individual development was needed to create insight into the flux and process of knowledge as well as a broader base of knowledge that could be applied when faced with business challenges – all of this was to create a learning-to-learn culture. Ultimately, this had to lead to the strengthening of the student's role as strategic partner and change agent within the organization.

The decision-making process that was needed to start a corporate MBA was very long. A variety of possibilities were discussed. One consisted of modules which were part of a horizontal (different topics, same level) as well as a vertical (increasing complexity within the same topic) development path. The added value of each alternative was then assessed in relation to the overall corporate strategy and vision. Eventually, the company decided to embark on a corporate MBA program, as part of an overall management human resources development initiative because the program would create the right level of skills, knowledge, and learning strategies that were decided on during the assessment. Particular modules from the MBA program could also be simplified and used in other development paths. In other words, these could 'cascade' into other either more basic or more specialized development programs. The cascading possibility was regarded as both an economic and a strategic move by the company, as it would result in faster future development and a multiple implementation of the modules at reduced cost.

The philosophy behind this program can be described as follows: merging management concepts with company-specific organizational and business themes, the creation of new behavior and a knowledge-generating culture, an evolution from routine to creativity, and entrepreneurship linked to the overall company vision. Management skills were used as a basis for the program design. By merging functional and behavioral areas, the creators of the program envisaged a generalist approach to management.

In our example, the company appointed an independent program coordinator who functioned as an interim manager. The coordinator's role was that of main designer, developer, and organizer of the program. He also liaised between the company and the educational providers (business schools and individual instructors from management institutes as well as the company), and between the students, the HR Department and management. He was also actively involved in the selection of the providers and of the students. Once the program started, he briefed instructors about the company and the program's philosophy, assessed course materials, and coached the students in their personal development.

The program was carefully designed to meet the company's objectives and cover its concepts, while adhering to the 80/20 rule where it concerned generic management concepts and specific critical issues. First, a number of concepts and techniques were introduced; then these were used to further discuss relevant issues and challenges for the company. At the same time, this approach created a balance between the company's strategic and operational levels. On a conceptual level, new and innovative models and concepts were used. This had an important impact on the selection of faculty staff and business institutes that were to participate in the program. Furthermore, the program was designed to increase the complexity of the issues, and therefore the ensuing discussion. As a direct result of the specific company context and needs, the program was given a European theme and strong strategic and marketing components. The European theme was reflected in every course. In addition, a specific European module was incorporated into the program. It covered the role and function of European institutes and the European Commission, as well as an introduction into European legislation, with a special emphasis on competition law.

Nearly two-thirds of the fifteen-month program was like a regular MBA program. The idea behind the consortium model – several affiliate organizations and several management institutes – was to provide the company's regional organizations with a Pan-European view, and mix this with different business education methods, and the approaches and expertise of several management institutes. The program's creators foresaw a true exchange of cross-cultural and cross-business experiences. An additional advantage was that no particular management institute dominated the program so that the company would not be solely associated with and dependent on the quality of a single management institute. Quality (content and logistics), location, facilities, and expertise in a particular field were key factors when choosing the participating management institutions.

After the company's decision to start a 'company MBA', the coordinator began a communication strategy intended to inform and motivate staff to join the program. Parallel to this, the company defined selection criteria similar to the typical MBA requirements, coupled to additional company-specific criteria. Throughout the selection procedure, candidates' supervisors were coached so as to ensure their active support in their role as mentor.

A kick-off weekend was organized two weeks prior to the 'official' start of the program. The weekend was seen as an important introductory phase for the participants. The coordinators were able to explain the content and organization of the program and started a discussion about participants' management' expectations. The participants also did a business simulation game to force them to think about the dynamics among different functionalities within a given organization. Team building, self-assessment and development were the central focus, as well as the facilitating role of the program coordinators. Participants also completed a management competency test, which provided them with a competency profile of themselves. They were given personal feedback by an expert and, after peer discussions and self-reflection, they had to write a personal development or learning plan that was aimed at developing certain skills that were essential for their individual career development and personal agendas.

The MBA program was altogether designed to avoid disruption of work activities, so as not to affect students' performance or to upset their managers and supervisors. Therefore, the first part of the program was based heavily on the use of technology, particularly electronic data transfer and print materials. For the same reason, the program designer incorporated a solid distance-learning aspect into the program. The distance-learning aspect included distance-teaching – the instructor's role in the process. Especially in the first part of the program – the basic courses – straight distance-learning was used: a combination of electronic instruction combined with paper-based learning, introducing mini-cases and additional reading and live and video-taped programming, supplemented by textbooks, computer programs, multimedia and other teaching materials (CD-ROM, simulations, etcetera). Individual tutoring was available when needed. Also, students could exchange information and experiences via Internet, or use it to find information. One-way interaction, standard lecturing of materials to all students, standard, structured practice, and instant, specific feedback and feed-forward were combined with learning at individual pace and based on individual time schedule.

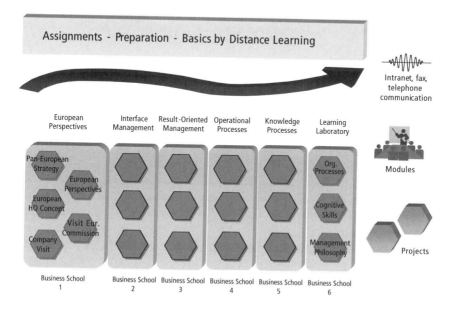

Figure 3.2 Model of a corporate MBA

The second part of the program followed what would be considered a more traditional attendance formula. Intensive one-week blocks took place in the partnering management institutes once every 6 weeks. In between two modules, students had to complete assignments and prepare the forthcoming module. The blocks were issue-based, multidisciplinary, and integrative. Self-assessment, peer-learning, project work and case building were all learning tools. Throughout the program, faculty staff from different disciplines acted as facilitators and coaches and held up mirrors to the students.

After about six months, the group was in need of an injection of energy and motivation, so an outdoor weekend was organized. The weekend focused on leadership and team-building exercises by means of an element of adventure as well as briefing and de-briefing sessions, coaching and camaraderie. In the end, it was not so much the 'adventure' that was important, as the application of conceptual thoughts and ideas to practical challenges, individual and group feedback, and professional coaching. The importance of the program coordinator was again quite evident as the coach in this rejuvenating weekend.

The final piece of the overall program jigsaw consisted of an action-learning graduating project, in which the participants had to act as internal consultants working on real-life issues. These projects made a contribution to the overall 'education' of the participants, as they made participants integrate conceptual knowledge with practical company experience, individual learning with team learning, and gather hands-on project management experience. These projects entailed real business development and strategic issues. This forced participants to identify academic and theoretical principles with which to implement solutions to managerial and business challenges. During the two to three-month projects, participants worked under the supervision of both an academic and a company advisor who guided students when they veered off into the wrong direction. The company also considered the projects to be a return-on-investment, as they were a highly visible, tangible and substantial contribution to overall organizational development – at relatively low cost, especially when compared to similar projects done by an outside consulting firm. Also implementation of the projects was quite in light of the fact that both during and after the project, several stakeholders of the project worked for the organization.

Information Technologies

As was argued earlier in this section, the uptake of corporate universities especially seems to be highly correlated to the development of technological possibilities for IT-based education. Not only do companies create more and more corporate universities, but they almost exclusively base them on an IT platform to facilitate knowledge and information sharing. They all seem to recognize the tremendous push that IT can present to corporate development activities. Nevertheless, most companies are aware of the need to view IT, in order to use it successfully in education, in the light of the overall corporate strategy.

With a remarkable sense of detail, Meister describes some IT experiences, mainly US ones. These experiences provide us, the authors, with some insight into the reasons for possible failure or success of our own efforts to explain the building of the Hybrid Business School in the next chapters.

Technology is considered to be an enabler to accelerate learning. Effective learning can only happen if the learning process is carefully tied to the strategic needs of the business. IT-based learning ideally caters to relatively 'flat' and flexible organizations. Successful experiments are often based on learning alliances, both within the company, and with outside partners. Corporate universities often operate as a business and therefore follow the rules of commercial feedback.

Corporate universities are more a process than a place. Of course, certain aspects of the educational process, such as face-to-face workshops and the university administration may call for actual buildings, but education itself is linked to the process and not to the physical place. Corporate universities link learning paths to employees' personal development, which is an interesting development pertaining to students' motivation and accreditation of learning. Employee self-development is often linked to compensation, and career self-management then becomes a further motivator for learning. This approach proves successful.

Corporate universities are also increasingly attracting the interest of both clients and suppliers of a company. Sometimes, there is a creation of 'communities-of-interest' around certain issues of common interest. Corporate universities equally fit the life-long learning need of individual employees. In order to cater to different stakeholder interests, programs offered by corporate universities often contain the three following areas: core workplace skills, corporate citizenship, and contextual issues.

What IT typically is intended for in corporate universities is the creation of a continuous open learning laboratory for the different stakeholders. Compared to regular universities, companies have a tendency to pay more attention to how technology transforms the learning process itself. Corporate virtual schools also pay a great deal of attention to an improved pedagogical approach, with the knowledge content of the courses getting second best. Although these virtual learning laboratories use advanced technologies such as satellite classes, multi-media on the network, video-conferencing and web-based teaching, they are not incorporated into the IT that is set up at the expense of the learning process itself. IT-based learning in companies does focus on the learning process on which the courses are based. The need for immediate applicability of learning seems to motivate corporate universities in exploring the learning metaphors more in depth, rather than to experiment with more fancy technology as a mere gadget. This economic need, i.e., the urge to be able to apply the acquired skills and knowledge immediately within the company, could be the main distinction between successful and failed experiments in on-line learning.

Let us have a closer look at how companies go beyond the regular university's scope, with the aim of fostering learning and knowledge sharing. The innovative uses of new technologies such as the Internet suggest the close link between the effort of a company to develop knowledge management and the emerging success of newly created corporate (virtual) universities.

The emergence of the Internet and intranet technologies opened a whole new perspective. In the majority of its educational applications, however, the Internet is solely used as a powerful resource for structuring the information and navigating the communication space. People often describe communication technologies in conduit terms, talking of information as being 'in' books, files, or databases, i.e., information that can just as easily be accessed or 'outsourced'. We are asked to put ideas 'down on paper', to 'send them along', and so forth. As the example of Duke showed, the Internet can also be a powerful resource for constructing and negotiating the social space. Scattered groups of people and individuals, unknown to one another, even living in contiguous areas, and sometimes never meeting, are nonetheless enabled to share social space. In the professional environment, this kind of self-created and self-organizing groups is new. A different appraisal of the working-learning-innovating triangle, however, supported by an informal IT platform, can lead to the development of a process called 'community-based knowledge refinement': an example of an emergent knowledge environment. Brown describes these organizations as 'communities-of-practice'.

Communities-of-practice can take different shapes. The first one is illustrated by the example of sales representatives. Sales representatives can form an on-line community of learning by sharing experiences. If a sales rep has a particular problem at a client's premises and he cannot immediately find a solution, he can consult the network and discuss this with colleagues. Interesting problems and cases remain stored in the database for future consultation. The same network or community is used for educational purposes and information sharing. Hansen and his colleagues describe a similar process of 'personalization' as a tool used by consultants at firms such as Bain & Co. or McKinsey & Co. These firms focus on dialogue between individuals rather than (codified) knowledge objects in a database. Using networks of expertise and checking a 'people finder' database, consultants can tap into a worldwide network of colleagues' experience. Knowledge is shared not only face-to-face but also by means of the telephone, e-mail, and video-conference.

Another form of a community-of-practice is one which is created around a common area of interest, for example diabetics. A community-of-practice would in this case be created around perhaps a pharmaceutical company, producing drugs for diabetics, a medical insurance company, medical staff and possibly the government. The common aim of the practice may be the provision of better and cheaper service for diabetics. This 'inter-organizational' community can exchange information, discuss, give advice, and so on, a win-win situation for all. Above all, this community creates knowledge by merely sharing experiences.

With his concept of communities-of-practice, Brown attempts to give an integrated view on working, learning and innovating within a particular corporate situation. The complexity of contradictory forces that put an organization's assumptions and core beliefs in direct conflict with members working, learning, and innovating, arises from a misunderstanding of the meaning of these three activities. The corporate tendency to down-skill can often lead to non-canonical practice (i.e., practice that is not described by rules and in manuals) and to the creation of communities being driven further underground so that the insights gained through work are hidden from the organization as a whole. Later changes or reorganizations, whether or not intended to down-skill, may disrupt what they did not know was there. The gap between hidden and actual practice may become too large to be bridge by non-canonical practices. To close that gap, an organization will need to reconceive of itself as a community-of-practice, acknowledging in the process the many non-canonical communities in its midst.

The company's size is not the single determining factor. Within an organization that is perceived as a collective of communities, and not simply of individuals, and in which experimenting is acceptable, separate community perspectives can be communicated. Out of this friction of competing ideas, improvized sparks of organizational innovation can emerge. Sources of innovation can also lie outside an organization, among its customers and suppliers.

The organizational design and the paths that link communities to one another could enhance a healthy autonomy of communities, while simultaneously creating an interconnectedness that helps disseminate separate communities' experiments. In some form or another, the stories that support learning-in-working and innovation should be allowed to circulate. The technological potential to support this distribution (e-mail, bulletin boards and similar devices) is available. Working-class groups, such as the reps, are remarkably open with one another and share knowledge. Within these communities, news travels fast and community knowledge is readily available to its members.

This view of communities-of-practice contrasts strongly with the perspective of the conventional workplace, where:
- Working and learning are laid down in formal descriptions so that people (and organizations) can be held accountable.
- Groups are organized to define responsibility.
- Organizations are given boundaries to enhance concepts of competition.
- Peripheries are closed off to maintain secrecy and privacy.

Whereas information technology has now become widely available and, particularly, the Internet has grown exponentially, the use of IT has not significantly progressed. It often simply reinforces the classical metaphor of knowledge being poured, by a teacher, into an empty vessel (the student). Little attention is paid to the reconceptualization of the traditional notions of teaching, instruction, the learner, subject matter, technology and the system, and transforming these. Even if an instructor did attempt to teach, it is not justifiable to conclude that nothing was learned. The process is not, then, like the addition of a brick to a building, where the brick remains as distinct and self-contained as it was in the bricklayer's hands. Instead, it is a little like adding color to color in a painting, where the color that is added becomes inseparably part of the color that was there before. What is learned can never be judged solely in terms of what is taught. This is a serious problem for the operationalization of situated learning, based within a framework of educational technology.

Rabindranath Tagore once introduced an interesting metaphor of 'stolen knowledge'.

> A very great musician came and stayed in [our] house. He made one big mistake … [he] determined to teach me music, and consequently no learning took place. Nevertheless, I did

casually pick up from him a certain amount of stolen knowledge.

Tagora 'stole' knowledge by watching and listening to the musician as the latter, outside his classes, played for his own and others' entertainment. Part of the need to 'steal' arises because relatively little of the complex web of actual practice can be made the subject of explicit instruction.

The work of Brown unfolds a rich and complex picture of what a situated view of learning needs do, and emphasizes in particular the social, rather than the merely physical nature of 'situatedness'. Legitimate peripheral participation (LPP), which is his definition of learning, clearly distinguishes between learning and intentional instruction. The richness of interpersonal interaction is usually either overlooked or deliberately disrupted in the classroom. In the workplace, learners can, when necessary, steal their knowledge from the social periphery, that consists of other, more experienced workers and ongoing, socially shared practice. The classroom, unfortunately, tends to be too well-secured against theft. Information technology should not reinforce the limitations of the classrooms, but rather allow for participative learning.

The particular example that Brown uses, is the one of 'Community-Based Knowledge Refinement' at Xerox. Web technology (http + html) made 'the network-of-networks', the Internet, accessible to a wider population. Within the view that innovation is in itself a joint activity of a number of 'Complex Adaptive Systems' (CAS), Internet and the web can provide a medium for innovation.

Technological companies do not focus on products anymore, but on product platforms. These especially designed product platforms also tap into the company's tacit knowledge. Each product platform can market a number of product variants. Furthermore, platforms themselves evolve through discontinuous changes in technology components. The role of the product platform can be compared to the role of the chromosome in the human being. To some extent, all companies have in their 'peripheries' (the frontline) real-time improvisations and experimentation. But very often they are not visible and therefore we cannot learn from them. In the first place, we need to learn in order to see the learning that takes place within these peripheries.

As Brown's research with sales representatives at Xerox shows, an important, non-documented copy quality fault is dealt with via 'story telling'. Since telling stories seems to enable people to learn, the task for information technology is to create a 'learning space' which allows self-learning through the exchange of stories. In IT terminology this could be called collaborative software.

Within Xerox, a process of Community-Based Knowledge Refinement has been introduced. This system filters the number of cases per product. Essentially, representatives produce some cases (stories) that are put up to a peer review process. Referees appointed by the community then judge the cases before they get integrated in the 'case base'. This mechanism triggers both social and technical learning. It is a social way to create and award good ideas. Particularly in technology-driven industries, the award winning aspect proves to be a motivator.

This case base is of immediate interest and use to the representatives, but it also allows further learning using learning algorithms. Genetic algorithms (based on sources of variability) are used to create a 'community mind'. Learning and adaptation, also in the 'community mind', takes place through critique, cross-coupling and combining 'tips'. With this approach, a vast space boils down to 'knowledge'.

The important question for a company is how to facilitate this process, and how to promote its emergence. In leveraging the small efforts of many (people) so as to stimulate learning and innovation, web technology can be especially useful. However, web technology needs to be specifically organized in order to be able to facilitate learning, and organizations seldom do this. Fortunately, 'emergent practice' can be identified through 'authorized practice'. It is only a different sub-set.

A comparable example is the one of the medical insurance company and the pharmaceutical company that together mediated a focus group for clients suffering from diabetes. This discussion forum is a self-organized group of people sharing an interest, but is facilitated by people from both companies. The companies provide the clients with information about how to improve their quality of life and well-being. Clients are happier because they are more informed and receive better service. The insurance company lowers its long-term expenses for diabetics, and the pharmaceutical company gains direct access to its clients. Hence, companies should in general attempt to identify the 'emergent' more quickly. It will contribute to core competencies, and as a whole, the company will become a powerful, innovative entity. It will stimulate the capacity of creating new businesses, core products, end products and services through the development of capabilities and recombining resources rather than fixing a few core competencies.

An interesting way to support the emergent or 'the social fabric' in companies is the use of hypertext technology within the framework of a 'knowledge refinement server'. In the case of Xerox, the knowledge refinement server allows people to contribute to, as well as to reflect and learn from, experiences and each other. The advantage of hypertext links is that they build on existing thoughts, provide comment, suggest new possibilities, and so on, comparable to the 'story telling' approach described earlier. (Cross-)linking comments or commenting on comments enables people to learn, but is also what hypertext can produce.

The formal organization and the formal IT support deal with classic documents and are based on a classic client/server document management system. The informal IT support deals with HTML-type documents, new expressive forms and a www-like community document system for which the Internet protocol is the backbone. The Intranet could even use synchronous multi-cast. Broadcast, midcast and narrowcast could be used in a synchronous and a-synchronous mode, both symmetrical and a-symmetrical. Rather than an infrastructure, it is a new (working) medium.

3-5 Educational Competency Approach

In reaction to, as well as in an attempt to do away with the criticisms of the business environment on management institutes, many institutes have incorporated the development of managerial competencies in their programs. In doing so, they aim to make the programs more practical. Business institutes in the US and Europe have created specific courses such as for example entrepreneurship, management communication, presentation skills, or integrated and multidisciplinary teambuilding modules. Didactic strategies such as business games and simulations, group work and peer review, debates and discussions, video-taping and coaching, personal journals and real-life consulting projects, are integrated in the curriculum to make business education more pragmatic.

As we have seen in an earlier section, the essence of the business world's criticism transcends the issue of pragmatism in business education. There are also clear business, organizational and managerial reasons to embed managerial competencies in business programs. Managerial skills reflect the different aspects of changed and changing managerial roles, i.e., having to deal with fragmentation and perplexing paradoxes, as well as daily routines. Herein lies the weakness of the 'mainstream' approach to managerial competencies, as was illustrated earlier. It is seen as a simple vehicle to increase the attraction of the program, lacking the depth of a true philosophy or clear broader framework. This philosophy on framework indeed echoes the essence of the managerial mindset.

As we concluded in the previous chapter, it is clear that no single concept of management captures the diversity of roles and activities in which managers are involved. As executives live within fragmented and discontinuous environments, and create complex corporate environments, they don not behave in systematic fashion. The need for multi-faceted knowledge, intelligence, and skills necessary to create progress – i.e., a flexible strategic vision, the organization's constant renewal – while being able to preserve the core becomes prevalent in management. Generic, organic and changing skills reflect the capacity for creating new businesses, core competencies, capabilities, products and services. It puts great emphasis on the ability of individuals to constantly learn about the environment, about their own performance, their objectives and capabilities, and in the light of this learning, to change, and to learn from the change. Based on this interpretation of managerial competencies, we will describe a framework and some underlying principles for an educational competency approach.

Competencies Framework

In the first place, and given the way the different competency dimensions have been defined, it is clear that . management programs such as degree programs will focus on developing generic competencies while only creating an awareness about changing competencies. All managers can apply generic competencies to organizations and different roles as they reflect the core of the managerial mindset, and of managerial and organizational life. Existing as they do across the organization in varying degrees of importance and mastery, they refer to more abstract competencies, to an epistemology of inquiry reflecting thought processes, a theory of practice, a deeper understanding of reflective practices, and critical distance. Because generic competencies offer this continuity, business institutes can especially focus in their degree programs on their development. As a consequence, generic competencies also have a long-term horizon: the ability to articulate a (shared) strategic vision, communicate and translate that vision throughout the organization, and enable organizational members to realize that vision is part of generic competence. The ability to encourage double-loop learning involving the ability to translate a managerial phenomenon into a conceptual level, come to an understanding, and translate that understanding back to a practical level, is another. Further illustrations are the ability to take critical distance, gathering patterns in order to understand managerial paradoxes, combining of resources and intellectual technologies.

'Changing competencies' and competencies of changeability cannot be overlooked in degree programs either. They include emerging, transitional, and maturing competencies, which refer to those competencies that that become increasingly relevant over the years (emerging), skills that become less relevant (maturing), or competencies whose relevance may decrease while their emphasis increases (transitional). Firstly, we tend to think about technology-related competencies due to the constantly changing nature of technology. Another example would competencies related to business development. It is important for participants and students to be aware of these time-related competencies; they are considered a source of competitive advantage connecting speed to strategic purposes, information, critical issues, and knowledge management. Also, it enables them to judge the impact of the non-linear and unpredictable fashion in which business moves rather than behaving in a risk-averse manner.

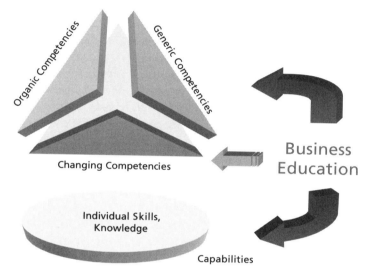

Figure 3.3 An educational competencies framework

Since organic competencies are defined as organization-specific, arising from a specific role itself (role-unique or context-specific), only company-tailored programs will be able to include them in their overall competency-approach. Company-specific programs can also create a more appropriate context, i.e. learning community, for instance to develop double-loop learning.

Managerial competencies are supported by capabilities. Capabilities for example describe the behavioral skills needed to communicate, to work as a member of a team, and to understand the dynamics of the context in which individual managers work. Capabilities such as personal effectiveness, negotiation skills, time management, team skills, cross-cultural awareness, or communication skills are fundamental as they allow people to develop competence. As a consequence, it is important that the development of capabilities is included in the competency-approach.

It is vital that business program designers should start with the development of a list of competencies. While professional literature or research can help to develop a list of generic competencies, organic competencies can be found by investigating the company's core competencies and capabilities, its culture and philosophy, its vision and long term strategies, and the target group's role. In other words, the list of organic competencies has to reflect the specifics of a particular company's business, organizational, professional, functional and managerial environments or contexts, as well as the particular roles of the target group. Also, competency lists only have added value if it is forward looking, reflecting the roles of today's as well as tomorrow's managers.

How can one proceed with these different dimensions and competencies? Competency lists tend to be quite specific: competencies should be described in detailed and descriptive ways, as well as in observable, behavioral terms. Effectively using logic and data analysis to make high-quality decisions, for example, can be seen as a behavioral descriptor for decision-making. Giving candid and constructive feedback is part of the competency of 'developing and motivating others'.

Next, competencies have to be clustered into key output areas, capturing a common denominator. Such a key output area could be customer orientation or business acumen. A final important element is prioritizing (by, for instance, allocating relative weight). Since any program will only offer a limited opportunity to develop competencies, program designers will have to prioritize and only implement a few competencies and capabilities in their programs according to their particular context. In this way, it will be clear to the participant what the focus of the program will be. The individual is thus enabled to customize the competencies and capabilities to suit his or her situation and stage of development, especially when the competencies list is combined with a self-development plan that will identify the student's skills and learning style.

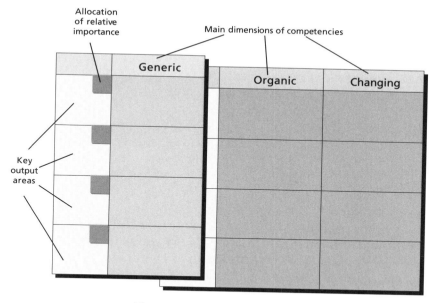

Figure 3.4 Competency table

The obvious challenge, now, is to ensure that these competencies are sufficiently embedded into every aspect (i.e., person) of the learning process, that is, they need to be consciously learned as opposed to assumed to be understood.

Specific Program Design and Program Philosophy

It is quite obvious that, depending on what program design one decides on, particular capabilities and competencies will be lost or enhanced. As a result, each program has a different value. Time management, for example, will more easily be developed in high-pressure MBA programs. In MBA programs that switch from 2 week of classes to a week of project and/or preparation work schedule, it will be harder to acquire a skill such as this. It all depends on the exact program philosophy and on program's aim. This goes hand in hand with a well-defined theme that should underlie and stream-line the whole program, as was mentioned before. This means a theme needs to really reflect the philosophy and design of a particular program.

Firstly, program design will enable the development of capabilities in support of the competencies. Given the prioritization of particular competencies, sessions can be organized to recognize, explain, develop, and experiment with these capabilities. But first, program designers will have to define the relevant capabilities are in the light of the list of competencies, and how these can be translated to an educational context, i.e., the learning process and sessions. These sessions could run parallel to or be integrated with other modules for which the skill or technique is particularly relevant. To illustrate the first approach, this could for example be some sessions on argumentation, communication, and negotiation techniques. At first, an introduction on argumentation theory could be given, followed by some showcases and discussions on its relevance and use in managerial communication. The next session would then look at argumentation theory from a methodological point of view, after which participants could do assignments and read texts on critical thinking, negotiation, and the evaluation of information. A third session would link argumentation and communication, after which a negotiation role-play could be staged. The play would be video-taped to be analyzed using self-confrontation techniques guided by the teacher. The last session would link argumentation with negotiation techniques after which the tape would be analyzed again. Also embedded into the process of the individual development plans are the feedback and extensive debriefing sessions from peers and staff. This is a continuous process, as the self-development path will be the leitmotiv for the entire program.

Competencies are more closely linked to program philosophy. The program philosophy will not only decide how management will be taught, but will also determine the conceptual angle managerial competencies are approached from. For instance, it will decide which competencies will take priority and how competencies are translated into observable, behavioral descriptors. The program philosophy will also reveal the platform that brings together knowledge and competencies. We have explained previously that many institutions have included more integrative clusters that weave together common themes from multiple and multi-disciplinary angles, and action-learning-based consulting projects. Others use a mixture of both approaches: 1. they will start with some functional courses, and move on to more integrative modules, then to applying integrative modules to conclude every semester, or 2. offering completely problem-based or issue-based programs. The competency approach explained here, however, is more closely related to a curriculum focusing on business processes. A focus on business processes will mean concentrating on the key factors to an organization's competitive advantage, newer management paradigms, organizational and strategic processes as the focal point of value creation and reinvention, and new economic, organizational and managerial realities. Consequently, it offers consistency between management philosophy, managerial roles, program philosophy, program design, managerial competencies, and the educational competency approach. As a result, the approach will be of greater added value.

Teaching and Pedagogical Philosophy

We stated earlier that educators should approach theories as reflection-in-action that will teach students to learn how to ask more pertinent questions. The answer lies in an overall teaching philosophy in which the art of inquiry based on working with 'best principles' is central. This will enable participants to take a critical distance and to push their limits. It will offer an ability to translate a managerial phenomenon to a conceptual level, come to an understanding, and translate that understanding back to a practical level. It is especially those shifts between levels that students have to master. Remember that managerial paradoxes reflect confusion or a collapse of different logical levels. Even though contradictions are inferred, they are not just referring to a simple contradiction. Paradoxes are *con-fusion*: the different levels cannot be reached because the fusion causes the differentiation of logical levels to disappear.

Learning is characterized by interpretation rather than by description and analysis. It is a journey through the real world, and through networks of meanings including aspects of self-knowledge, self-criticism, and self-development. As a consequence, teachers have to act as mentors, facilitators and helpers. At times they will have to take an almost Socratic role and provide dialog, and guide participants through the journey of dynamics turbulence and complexities by asking pertinent questions. By means of a subtle mixture of coaching, negotiated authority and 'learned freedom', the teacher sometimes takes responsibility for learning while sometimes this responsibility is shifted to the students. Students have to be made aware of underlying dynamic movements and taught to look beyond the obvious and trivial. They have to learn to develop a feel for complexities and issues, to analyze managerial or organizational phenomena while keeping a critical distance in order to reflect.

In short, the answer does not lie in the business simulations, personal journals, peer reviews, specific team-building and leadership modules, multi-disciplinary case studies or computer simulations. These are simple tools to create a testing and experimentation laboratory. It is important, however, that these tools are used to develop a particular competency. In other words, teachers will have to focus on the development, and assessment of that competency within the broader context of the program's overall aims. They will have to identify appropriate tools for the competencies that were identified and prioritized. This can either be done parallel certain modules, or as an integration.

Another element in the teaching philosophy is the examination of competing theories and reference frames. This will create a plurality of discourses and mindsets rather than reducing students' perceptions to a single all-including grand 'master theory', and will result in a more critical and integrative insight. As theories reflect networks of intelligibility, knowledge, experience and meanings, they are vehicles used to examine the boundaries and limitations of knowledge. Hence, the educational community should see theories as potential ways to create new possibilities.

Teachers will have to lobby for support for the development and application of such a philosophy. 'Teaching teacher' seminars, the development of databases consisting of educational materials, and attracting employees who are experienced in using these, can help departments to embrace and implement such an overall teaching philosophy. Actually, it not only portrays a philosophy towards management education, teaching and learning (i.e., the pedagogical metaphor and ways to understand learning), or towards the kind of learning community that has to be created, but it also describes a managerial mindset that one wants the students and participants to develop. It is also material to ensure support for faculty focusing on the didactic approach. For instance, as co-teaching is one strategy, staff and faculty will have to coordinate efforts and have to be coached in order to find the right balance and in order to ensure open minds.

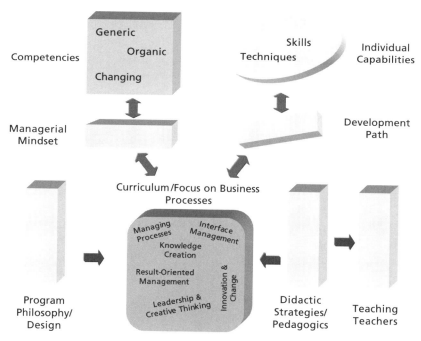

Figure 3.5 An educational competency approach

It is clear that the implementation of such a competency approach is labor intensive and demanding. It might even lead to reducing the number of topics that are taught in a program. The added value of the competency approach, however, is also demonstrated by reduction of class sizes. That is why it is especially geared to executive education. Last but not least, it will also be important to include an assessment on the competency development.

3-6 Building Stones for the Hybrid Business School

- Management education can be seen as an important vehicle in developing 'emergent' strategies, and managing knowledge as well as the organization's capabilities that trigger organizational learning. Therefore, it is crucial for management education and knowledge management to be harmonized.
- The dominant paradigm of management education is not entirely relevant to the needs of graduates, and hence does not prepare them for their managerial roles.
- No single best way of teaching exists, no single best way of learning can be identified. Learning remains very much a free act of individuals.
- Subject matter is not an objective pre-set body of transferable knowledge.
- The Hybrid Business School is founded on a combination of the 'traveling' and 'growing' pedagogic paradigms. The travelling metaphor advocates a more holistic and self-organizing principle. It is the learner who is in charge of his or her learning process. The growing metaphor, then, focuses on personality development. Subject matters are seen as a set of experiences each student should absorb.
- We are convinced that the future of 'the' business school will mean curricula focusing on business processes and progressing towards the use of a learning laboratory.
- A learning community is a vehicle for sharing experiences, information, ideas, and knowledge, for developing an insight into patterns, and where resources and intellectual technologies are combined. Within this learning community, members participate as partners in a joint undertaking to advance learning and therein shape educational provision. Members will also receive moral and emotional support for learning.
- Technology is considered to be an enabler that accelerates learning. Effective learning can only take place if the learning process is carefully tied to the strategic needs of the business.
- An integrated view on the working-learning-innovating triangle in a particular corporate situation, supported by an informal IT

platform, can lead to the development of a process called 'community-based knowledge refinement'.

References

- Beck, J. (1994). *The New Paradigm of Management Education. Management Learning*, 25, 2, pp. 231-247.
- Brown, J. S. (1998). *Internet Technology in Support of the Concept of 'Communities-of-Practice': The Case of Xerox. Accounting, Management and Information Technologies*, 8.
- Brown, J. S. & Duguid, P. (1994). *Organizational Learning and Communities-of-Practice: Toward a Unified View of Working, Learning and Innovation.* In: H. Tsoukas, *New Thinking in Organizational Behaviour.* Oxford: Butterworth-Heinemann.
- *Business Week*, (1997), *Corporate America Goes to School.*
- *Business Week*, (1997), *When the best B-School is no B-School.*
- *Business Week*, (1997), *The Hottest Campus on the Internet.*
- Daniel, J. (1996). *Mega-Universities and Knowledge Media.* Kogan Page.
- Illich, I. (1972). *Deschooling Society.* Marian Boyars.
- Lundberg, C. (1993). *On the Dilemmas of Managerial Instruction.* Atlanta – August 1993. Academy of Management Annual Meeting.
- Meister, J. (1998). *Corporate Universities: Lessons in Building a World-Class Work Force.* McGraw-Hill.
- Raelin, J. A. (1994). *Whither Management Education? Management Learning*, 25, 2, pp. 301-317.

Chapter 4

Information and Knowledge
Technologies for Virtual Education

In the previous chapters, some insight has been given into the processes of learning and knowledge transfer. Figure 2.7, re-introduced below as figure 4.1, showed a schematic and therefore somewhat limited view on the processes of learning and knowledge management.

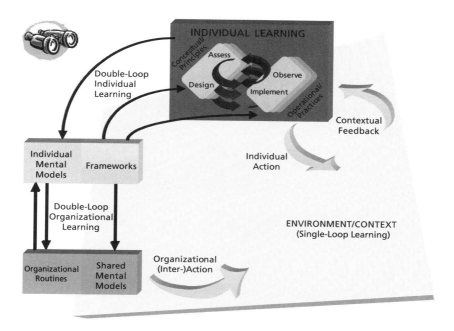

Figure 4.1 An integrated model of organizational learning

At this stage, we would like to take a more technological stance and discuss the information and knowledge technologies that support both knowledge management and virtual education. A remarkable and interesting overlap became obvious while we are attempting to realize and operationalize these processes with the necessary IT support.

On a conceptual level, knowledge management and virtual education will not be considered as two separate activities any more. The left-hand part of figure 4.1, as was argued earlier, describes (tacit) knowledge management. The right-hand part, on the other hand, describes virtual education. The overlap of both proves to be the flywheel engine that brings both knowledge management and virtual education to a higher level and closer to the corporate practice. The added value is created by combining the two. This overlapping construction, which we will call the Hybrid Business School, reinforces both knowledge management and virtual education.

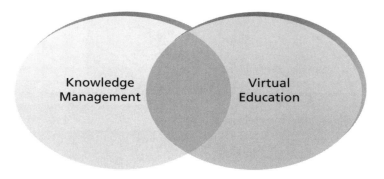

Figure 4.2 The overlap of knowledge management and virtual education

The result of this overlap is a textbook example of a '1 + 1 = 3' logic. On the knowledge management side, it allows us to deal especially with tacit knowledge while still being able to use the potential of explicit knowledge sharing (virtual education). On the virtual education side, it enables us to offer individualized continuous life-long-learning development paths to employees, with company-specific course material. Education should be considered to be integrative rather than specialized (i.e., knowledge of marketing, finance, etcetera). In other words, our view breaks with the popular trend of offering more and more specialized courses. We claim that specialization does not interest companies. Management is integration, is knowledge and skills within a given context. Just as information is meaningless without action, knowledge and skills are useless outside of a context. Technology is the factor that makes the difference. This approach to virtual education goes far beyond that of web-based teaching in which for example the Duke University and the University of Phoenix have excelled.

In this chapter, we will introduce the information and knowledge technologies necessary and available for building the Hybrid Business School: a technology-based approach to integrated (tacit) knowledge management and constant in-company learning. The conceptual frame we used to implement technology is the one shown in figure 4.1. We shall begin by schematizing this figure further in order to clarify goals, attributes and processes.

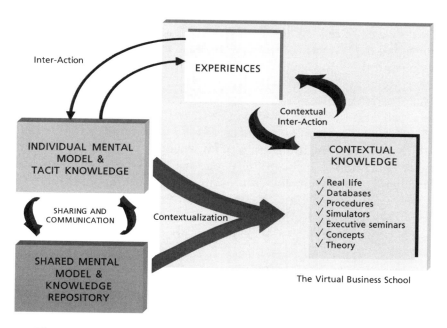

Figure 4.3 A schematic model of knowledge creation and learning

Figure 4.3 focuses on the information and communication flows and attributes that are seen to materialize in figure 4.1. All learning is begun by means of individual experiences. On the one hand, experiences interact with the individual mental models and thereby create tacit knowledge; on the other hand, experiences interact with contextual knowledge both as input and as a product of its interaction. Individual mental models (images) interact with each other in order to generate shared mental models and contribute to the knowledge repository. The latter process is organized by means of communication platforms. The process of interaction between experiences, tacit knowledge and knowledge repository, which is called the knowledge management process, links up with contextual knowledge. These links are attempts to contextualize some of the tacit knowledge in order to make it accessible to others. They feed the virtual learning process with part of the individual and corporate tacit knowledge.

The process of dealing with contextualized knowledge and experiences, based on an information and communication platform, is what we call the Virtual Business School, as on the right hand side of figure 4.3. The process of dealing with experiences, tacit knowledge and the knowledge repository is what we call the 'Knowledge Management Approach', depicted on the left-hand side of figure 4.3. The experiences that are exchanged between the two, the contextualization of tacit knowledge and the interaction between explicit knowledge and experiences, all on a continuous and integrated basis, trigger the integration of knowledge management and virtual education. This can only be realized when based on an adequate information and communication platform, preferably in a learning environment. Generally, integrating knowledge technologies and learning technologies use communication technologies, such as the Internet, group decision support systems, etcetera.

At this point, we would briefly like to introduce the more important knowledge technologies pertaining to knowledge management and virtual education.

4-1 Knowledge Management Technologies

It is a known fact that it is simple but not easy to create a learning/knowledge-based organization. The latest wave of information technology can be of help in creating knowledge-based/learning organizations. New developments in IT such as case-based reasoning systems (CBRS), group-decision support system (GDSS) and artificial neural networks can be of help in creating certain aspects of organizational learning processes and organizational transformation. We can only explain these technologies in passing here.

Case-Based Reasoning Systems (CBRS)

CBRS essentially consists of a case of library and a software system for retrieving and analyzing the comparable cases and associated information. The case library may consist of cases covering a broad range of ideas across different industries and businesses. Each case may contain a description to capture the underlying competitive situation, type of setting, management priorities, values that helped a certain strategy to succeed, and moments of learning. A software system helps to index each case in such a way that a search yields a number of 'similar cases'. The system can supply a complete explanation of the 'reasoning' that led to the results. If there is no case that matches the given situation exactly, then the system selects the most similar case. An adaptation procedure can be encoded in the form of adaptation rules. The result of the case adaptation is a completed solution, but it also generates a new case that can be automatically added to the case library.

The fact that the system has been exposed to cases previously makes it even more useful, as it encodes the important learning and thinking that went into previous decisions. As CBRS can generate details regarding justification for particular decisions and explanation for failures, it could be a support tool for a learning organization. It can be used as a learning device, but also as an input device for a knowledge base. Companies use this technology as a database of 'best practices'. It makes 'live experiences' accessible for others. However, what we are really looking for is 'best principles'. In many respects, compared to a database, CBRS is a static tool. The use of CBRS, however, as part of the knowledge management cycle as well as the case input of a virtual learning environment, allows us to go beyond the static situation: the process of learning and knowledge building is what helps develop best principles.

Group Decision Support Systems (GDSS)

Participatory management methods are increasingly gaining in interest in the corporate world. Japanese management methods and Dutch management practice have in common that traditionally, management by consensus is practised. Consensus management has lead to a more teamwork-type working environment, the formation of committees or working groups in which members share their knowledge so as to solve complex and structural problems. Referring to figure 4.3, participative decision-making contributes to the creation of mental models, both on an individual and a shared level, out of individual experiences. On the individual level, a GDSS can be used as a tool to help to structure a mental model or a routine, based on lived experiences. On a group level, the act of sharing and exchange allows for learning as a group, too, but it also creates further input in the sense that experiences lived by others are used as input data for an individual's mental model. One can see the immediate application in the sharing of ideas, and therefore in the creation of a group's shared mental model. This process of group learning also concerns the individual, and is therefore a useful tool for individual learning, but it does not focus solely on this.

Participative strategy formation is a learning process, as the various interest groups within an organization have different perceptions. Some group members may have more knowledge, competence and experience. Group learning occurs as soon as the interaction among members takes place. As one member shares knowledge with the other members in the group, the latter start collecting information and knowledge. The contextual feedback is of instant added value for all involved: each group learns and creates knowledge using its new knowledge base, while the base itself also evolves. Exponential and non-linear growth occurs when sharing group's knowledge base.

Sometimes, participative or group planning fails, due to a lack of proper participation, communication and understanding among the members of the group. Recent developments in information technology have provided systems such as Group Decision Support Systems (GDSS). A group decision support system (GDSS) is a computer-based system consisting of software, hardware, language components, procedures and tools to support participative strategy formation. There can be many different configurations of GDSS. These systems are there to aid for group planning.

GDSS enables a group to work interactively using the networked hardware and software to complete the various aspects of the business process. For example, automated brainstorming tools can be used to address questions such as 'what should the company do to become a knowledge-based/learning company within the next five years?' Using the system, group members can generate and evaluate relevant ideas from their individual terminals. The group facilitator can then prioritize the ideas they have generated and can select one for further electronic discussion. Finally, the group can work together using a text editor to formulate a policy statement regarding the goal they have selected.

The possibilities of existing GDSS vary. They essentially reduce communication barriers by providing technical features such as the display of ideas, voting, compilation, anonymous input/interaction, decision modeling, electronic mail and the bulletin board function. Also, they act as group experts by providing advice in selecting and arranging the rules that are to be applied during the decision-making process. The ultimate aim of this technology is to bring people together and facilitate efficient and effective interactive sharing of information among group members.

Today, intranets are replacing GDSS, particularly in their function of a communication device. If the learning is focused on the decision-making process, however, GDSS fulfills the purpose better than does an intranet.

Artificial Neural Networks

Artificial neural networks (ANNs) are a tool derived from artificial intelligence (AI). ANNs are also part of a new information-processing paradigm that simulates the human brain. It is a tool that excels in pattern-finding and structuring, without any prior information. It allows for the structuring of tacit knowledge, without making it explicit, but nevertheless making it accessible. ANNs are a vehicle for creating 'best principles' out of 'best practices'. Through learning and developing an epistemology of inquiry, practices can be understood at the level of principles. When a CBRS contains many cases and a query would generate an excessive number of cases, there should be a filter to break them down and summarize the cases. In essence, ANNs are instrumental in creating tacit knowledge out of stored experiences.

In this section, ANNs will be positioned a learning tool within the context of Information and Knowledge Technologies (IKTs). ANNs can contribute to the creation of tacit knowledge models, without making tacit knowledge explicit, but with the ability to make that knowledge potentially available to the company (see figure 4.3). ANNs are represented by the left-hand and middle part of figure 4.3. Though other advanced AI tools could be of help here, the use of ANNs has already been successful as a knowledge generating tool to support brand management, in visualizing a change management process, and in identifying client profiles. The combined use of CBRS and ANNs would create a strong backbone for a knowledge network, particularly in the light of the move towards world mass-individualization. Though ANNs cannot generate explanation at intermediate stages, integrating them with expert systems could somewhat alleviate this deficiency which would make them suitable for supporting the learning process.

4-2 Virtual Learning Technologies

The technology available for building a virtual learning environment is quite similar to that for creating a knowledge approach. The knowledge approach and the pedagogical effort reinforce each other, it is clear that the same technologies and technological platforms could be used.

Certain technologies, however, are particularly suitable for developing learning environments. The best known examples are Lotus Learning Space (based on a Lotus Notes platform), MLT (based on the Microsoft Exchange platform) and OLA of Oracle, to name but a few. An adequate learning environment needs to comply with a minimum number of conditions; for example, it should at least be able to produce the right kind of pedagogical material.

A few of the necessary conditions for a learning environment are listed here:

- A scheduler or agenda for the learner, which can be used by both tutor and student. This schedule will act as a guideline, but it will also monitor both progress and results.
- A media center of resources with hypertext links to.
- Managerial concepts (independent of functional areas).
- Case studies and applications.
- Managerial competencies (or definitions thereof).
- Other resource material.

The media center should include multi-media such as text, pictures, movies, digital videos, etcetera.

- An electronic course room for debating, question and answer sessions, and joint work, which will be the meeting place of the knowledge network that is created around the learning process ('communities-of-practice'). Here students, practitioners and faculty members will discuss topics of interest, sharing experiences, and jointly working on new cases. On a purely corporate level, an example would be the diabetic community that was mentioned earlier, where patients, medical staff, a pharmaceutical company, and a medical insurance company exchange information and knowledge.
- Profiles of students and tutors. Especially in a virtual environment, it is important to describe participants and their qualities in order to formulate networks. It would be difficult to work, via a network, with colleagues of whom you have no knowledge or history.
- An assessment manager. The assessment manager has dual responsibilities. In degree courses, it is imperative to measure learning. Via a personal development path, the assessment manager will work using a framework that is the corporate appraisal system, as well as the overall human resources management strategies and policies.

The Internet (or intranet) can help with one or more of the above-mentioned tasks. However, integrated software has the benefit it can integrate the student's environment, as well as being easy to use for both student and developer (or tutor). Integrated software is quicker to start up, and its users are generally more satisfied. In theory, it is possible for a virtual school to construct its own compatible software, but in practice, this is a difficult and complex undertaking and it often prevents a virtual school from going beyond offering a few electronic course or creating a discussion platform.

The database of pedagogical material should be linked to relevant web pages, with additional material or further networks of shared interest. Links can be made between the learning environment and a few relevant websites, e.g., to those of companies discussed during cases, or to company web sites containing relevant up-to-date study material, thus taking advantage of the wealth of information on the internet.

Video-conferencing is also an important and interesting technology. There is still a long way to go until video-conferencing will be reliable enough and can be optimally used for learning, but it has great future potential. Video-telephony, on the other hand, seems a very useful technological tool, especially for tutoring. Today video-telephony using the Internet is still slow, yet actually being able to see one's fellow student or tutor does add value to the conversation.

The most likely reason for the low level of satisfaction and limited success of video-conferencing is the dominant pedagogical metaphor, i.e., the transfer metaphor, that applies to teaching via video-conferencing. Video-conferencing attempts to deliver, in the same inefficient way as an attendance course, to various people in different locations. The use of video-conferencing (or video telephony) for communication and discussion purposes, as opposed to one-way broadcasting, has not been wide-spread so far. It requires advanced and expensive technology and is not yet within the average student's reach (be it on an individual or corporate level). Expensive and large equipment is needed for multi-point video-conferencing, which limits the 'time and space' in which courses can be delivered. As a result, video-conferencing is still rarely used. However, this situation is likely to change in the near future.

4-3 Communication Technologies

In order to meet the needs of both knowledge management and management learning, not only is an adequate stand-alone IT environment needed, but so is communication technology. Figure 4.3 highlights the importance of communication between the different areas. Each arrow can only be realized by using communication technology. Some technological tools for communication have already been discussed, but we cannot ignore the most popular technological tool, the Internet.

Intranets, based on Internet technology, are used in most major companies, mainly as a tool for enhancing communication. Internet and intranets can also fulfil the role of a communication platform for our purposes, if the necessary pedagogical material has been embedded. Ideally, a good learning platform should have its own communication facilities, or, if the learning platform and the communication facilities are separate, they should be integrated by dynamic links (comparable to Internet hypertext links). Arguably, it would be preferable to install communication platform(s) and learning environment(s) independently from one another, which would enhance flexibility and inter-operability. There is not a single best practice, but rather a few. Many companies are developing communication platforms based on Microsoft Exchange or Lotus Notes. This choice is perfect for learning environments such as Microsoft Learning Technology or Lotus Learning Space.

Group Decision Support Systems (GDSS, as discussed before) can partly play the same role; however, they make for a more restricted communication platform than does the Internet. The prime aim of a GDSS is not to provide a discussion platform, but in a case in which it were installed company-wide, it might not be necessary to replace it, but rather to integrate it in the learning environment.

The same can be said about chat-box or bulletin board facilities that some companies may have available. It is not advisable to have a discussion platform and learning materials separated in different software environments, but if there are platforms of any kind already available, one should concentrate on the functionality of that discussion forum and compare functionality to easiness of use, before taking any decision on the installation of new software.

Face-to-face communication should not to be forgotten. Even in a virtual business school, sit-in sessions, workshops and seminars are still an important part of the learning process. Certain aspects of a virtual business school, such as competency-driven learning, cannot be attained in a virtual environment. Face-to-face communication still proves to be most efficient and effective. Workshops, however, should concentrate on providing dialog rather than one-way communication.

As we argued previously, because of the changing economic and management environment, the development of management competencies have become crucial to the success of management today. It is not uncommon to find that concepts and cases are more geared towards supporting the knowledge-based side of education, whereas different types of cases, tutorials, project work and other activities are more supportive of competency-based education. Our concept of the Hybrid Business School calls for a balance between competencies and knowledge.

4-4 The Big Picture

The 'big picture', consisting of an integrated knowledge management and virtual education approach, designed for practicing managers, is what we will call the Hybrid Business School. This concept will be developed further in the next chapter. The overlap between knowledge management and virtual education, as illustrated in the figure below, creates leverage for both, provided both are adequately supported by information technology. It is this information technology point of view – one could almost call it a 'technology push' view – which allows us to create this 'Hybrid Business School leverage' for companies. In this section, we will discuss the information technologies necessary to realize both concepts as well as the overlapping leverage.

The integrated approach will allow for future availability of individual personal learning plans, or a 'mass-individualization' of management education based on dynamic employee profiles and career path necessities. In the end, the main agent for the Hybrid Business School is the organization and how it deals with managing the new economy, i.e., its philosophy, vision, strategies, managerial roles, alliances, etcetera, as was discussed in previous chapters. As a result, successful companies of the future will be learning organizations, whose learning aspects will be reflected in its core values, business strategy, training and development, HRD strategies, and HR policies. These elements are the constant agents of change and of knowledge management, and will constantly revise the company's management education, which is where the real added value of the Hybrid Business School lies.

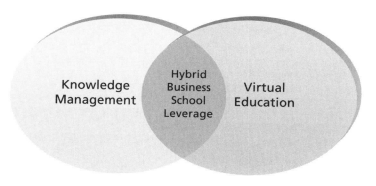

Figure 4.4 The Hybrid Business School's added value

The knowledge and learning potential of the Hybrid Business School approach lies mainly in its communication part. The existence of the repository, or of a CBRS, and ANNs or electronic pedagogical material is a necessary condition, although in itself, it does not suffice. Communication makes the creation and exchange of knowledge possible. This particular communication paradigm differs from most business schools' traditions, even from those that experiment with Internet-based courses. Although figure 4.5 depicts information technology in support of communication, it is the quality and the density of the communication itself that is the distinctive factor, especially because of the important and different communication that is played by in the 'travelling' and 'growing' paradigms.

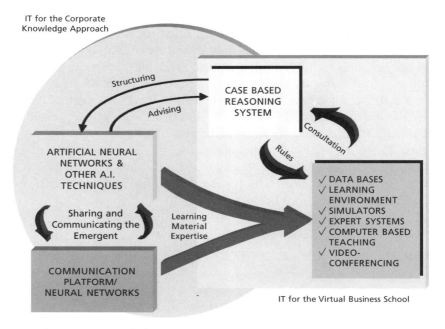

Figure 4.5 Knowledge technologies for the virtual business school

The Hybrid Business School is founded on a combination of the 'travelling' and 'growing' paradigms. As was discussed in the previous chapter, the travelling metaphor advocates a self-organizing principle. It is the learner who is in charge of his or her learning process, which the teacher taking the role of the experienced and expert leader who guides the students through unknown terrain. The teacher/guide not only leads the way, but also provides navigation tools and techniques, or maps and compasses. Hence, a more holistic view and the self-organizational character of learning are emphasized. The 'growing' metaphor, then, brings in the aspect of personality development. Rather than creating a body of knowledge, which would define the profession of management as is done by the professional approach, subject matters are seen as a set of experiences each student should incorporate into his or her personality. As a result, communication makes a crucial difference between the power of the 'travelling' and 'growing' paradigms and the (mainstream) transfer paradigm. A second important difference, at least in practice, is that the transfer paradigm is often part of functional and specialized courses, whereas the 'travelling' and 'growing' metaphors will be used to instill a more broader and integrated insight.

In practice, each Hybrid Business School project will need a different IT infrastructure. Figure 4.5 lists the building blocks for such a project. The more a business school or company manages to build an infrastructure as is depicted in figure 4.5, and fill it with the necessary information, the better it will be armed to undertake other Hybrid Business School projects. More than anything else this infrastructure offers flexibility. If a business school manages to develop pedagogical material and the necessary communication environment for running a particular degree program, they will also be able to easily and swiftly organize, for example, a two-week course in supply chain management, for any particular company. The richer the pedagogical base, the more flexibility.

4-5 Building Stones for the Hybrid Business School

- The process of dealing with contextualized knowledge and experiences, based on an information and communication platform, is what we call the Virtual Business School. The process of dealing with experiences, tacit knowledge and the knowledge repository, is what we call the 'Knowledge Management Approach'.
- If knowledge management and virtual education overlap, they are each lifted to a higher plane that is closer to the corporate practice. The Hybrid Business School reinforces both knowledge management and virtual education.
- New developments in IT such as Case-Based Reasoning Systems, Group Decision Support Systems and Artificial Neural Networks, can be used to support certain aspects of both the organizational learning process and organizational transformation.
- The organization is the real driver for the Hybrid Business School in the way it deals with managing in the new economy, i.e., its philosophy, vision, strategies, managerial roles, alliances, and so on.

Chapter 5

The Concept of
the Hybrid Business School

In this chapter, we will be developing in more detail the concept of the Hybrid Business School. When referring to the Hybrid Business School, we mainly relate to the single-loop learning cycle, as is depicted in the right-hand side of the by now well-known figure below. At the same time, the Hybrid Business School also is an important enabler for organizational double-loop learning.

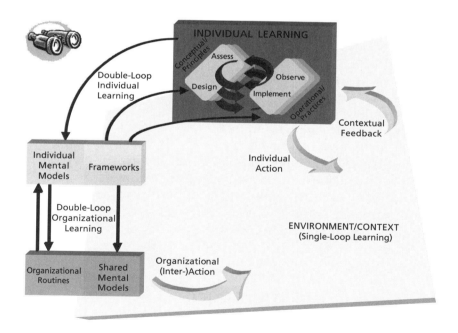

Figure 5.1 An Integrated Model of Organizational Learning

5-1 The Hybrid Business School's Building Stones

We have been guiding the reader through a variety of issues related to the idea of the Hybrid Business School, reflecting on the impact of the new economy on organizations and their processes, information and knowledge, managerial roles and competencies, management education and learning. These issues are here regarded as the building stones of the Hybrid Business School. Let us briefly list them here in more detail:.

- The high frequency with which radical and dramatic innovations occur, has resulted in a competitive accelerator and steeper business cycles – making time and speed crucial factors in competition, and forcing companies into quantitative and qualitative leaps of improvement.
- There's a rapid transition from an industrial society to a knowledge society.
- Information is a dynamic process. Knowledge is concerned with the way one learns to fix the flow of the world in temporal and spatial terms.
- Business, markets, and organizations change in a discontinuous, non-linear and dynamic way, allowing for the possibility of emergent and self-organizing behavior. Emergence cannot be predicted or even 'envisaged' using the knowledge of the function of each component in a system.
- No single definition of management can capture the diversity of roles and activities in which managers are involved.
- The ability of an organization to take effective action is based on tacit corporate knowledge. Knowledge management attempts to make this tacit knowledge explicit in order to share it.
- Managerial competencies reflect the particularities of managerial roles. Managerial competencies are sustained through continuous learning.
- Management education is an important vehicle for the development of 'emergent' strategies, and the management of knowledge and of those organizational skills that stimulate organizational learning. Therefore, it is crucial that management education and knowledge management are harmonized.

- The dominant paradigm of management education is not entirely relevant to the needs of graduates, and hence does not prepare them for their managerial roles.
- There is no single best way of teaching and no single best way to learn. Learning remains very much an act of free will.
- Subject matter is not an objective pre-set body of transferable knowledge.
- The Hybrid Business School is founded on a combination of the 'travelling' and 'growing' pedagogic metaphors. The 'travelling' metaphor advocates a more holistic and self-organizing principle. It is the learner who is in charge of his or her learning process. The 'growing' metaphor, then, focuses on personality development. Subject matters are seen as a set of experiences that each student should absorb.
- We are convinced that the future of 'the' business school will be curricula focusing on business processes that progress towards the use of a learning laboratory.
- A learning community is a vehicle for sharing experiences, information, ideas, and knowledge, for recognizing patterns, and combining resources and intellectual technologies. Within this learning community, members function as partners in a joint undertaking that advances learning, and therein shape educational development. Members will also be given moral and emotional support for learning.
- Technology is considered enabler to accelerate learning. Effective learning can only occur if the learning process is carefully tied to the strategic needs of the business.
- An integrated view on the working-learning-innovating triangle in a particular corporate situation, supported by an informal IT platform, will lead to the development of a process called 'community-based knowledge refinement'.
- The process of dealing with contextualized knowledge and experiences, based on an information and communication platform, is what we call the Virtual Business School. The process of dealing with experiences, tacit knowledge and the knowledge repository is what we call the 'knowledge management approach'.
- The overlap of knowledge management and virtual education lifts both knowledge management and virtual education to a higher plane and closer to corporate practice. The Hybrid Busi-

ness School reinforces the use of knowledge management and virtual education.

- New developments in IT such as Case-Based Reasoning Systems, Group Decision Support Systems and Artificial Neural Networks can be used in support of certain aspects of organizational learning processes and organizational transformation.
- The organization acts as the real driver for the Hybrid Business School, in the way it deals with managing in the new economy, i.e., its philosophy, vision, strategies, managerial roles, alliances, and so on.

5-2 The Concept of the Hybrid Business School

The essence of the Hybrid Business School should balance between two dimensions. On the one hand, there is the delivery dimension, which is the balance between virtual and non-virtual or face-to-face delivery and opportunities for dialogue. On the other hand, there is the content-driven dimension, reflected by the balance between corporate knowledge management and management development strategies, more generic business, organizational and managerial processes, and the development of managerial competencies. This is exactly why the Hybrid Business School is called hybrid; it is heterogeneous in every sense.

The Hybrid Business School's Content Dimension

The Hybrid Business School's content dimension is determined by the pedagogical metaphor on which it is based. The 'travelling' and 'growing' metaphors embrace self-organized learning which, as we have argued earlier, is a type of learning that is often successful in animal groups. As it is learner-centered, it enables the individual to learn at his own pace and in his own style, while allowing each person to explore in the depth and breadth necessary. The Hybrid Business School perspective focuses on individualized learning that is based on previous knowledge and experience, as well as the present job and specific needs. This element means that learning is not abstract but contextual as well as flexible: it happens at the appropriate time, in the appropriate dose, combined with an actual experience so that it can be immediately applied. This explains why the added value of the Hybrid Business School consists of creating an edge and in integrating corporate knowledge management, management development strategy, as well as human resource management. The latter embeds, amongst others, management development in the framework of a reward system that is toward creating a learning-to-learn culture, and also joins career development to employability. A better and closer fit of knowledge management, human resource management and learning creates an upward spiral in organizational learning.

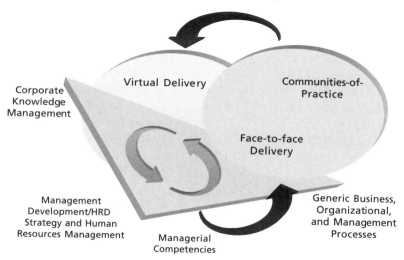

Figure 5.2 The Hybrid Business School dimensions

At the same time, our perspective embraces the non-linearity and dynamism of learning processes. The responsibility for the learning process is mainly the learner's, as individual mental models are only created through individual learning experiences. Learning does not does not happen because of a pre-set and fixed body of knowledge, but it enables the learner to discover and find appropriate information, i.e., to form his own body of knowledge using a hypertext platform. Clearly, it is the learner who defines what is 'appropriate'. The hypertext platform, which we will explain in more detail later, also accommodates a multitude of learners and myriads of learning paths.

The Overall Learning Strategy

Content and delivery are merged in the Hybrid Business School's overall learning strategy. Central is the integrated curriculum that focuses on business, organizational and strategic processes. This ensures both breadth and depth of the programs. The breadth is caused by the integration of issues with processes, the depth by the fact the learner can decide to acquire more in-depth knowledge or information about particular subjects. The curriculum design is supported by various types of information.

The Conceptual Level

First and foremost, the conceptual level provides a common language, a learning base which reflects the minimum level of a manager's knowledge. He or she should at least be able to translate a managerial phenomenon to a conceptual level, come to an understanding by asking pertinent questions, and translate that understanding back to a practical level. This will help develop critical distance. The learning base will be formed by corporate knowledge management and concepts related to the processes that are part of the curriculum. Because of its approach, the Hybrid Business School concept can be modular, and these modules can 'cascade' into different development paths. This approach offers flexibility in design, development, skill, scale, timing, and integration, apart from being more economical.

Reflection-in-Action

It is important, however, to look beyond the content of knowledge and treating it as a simple informational commodity, and to also focus on the dynamic process. Therefore, 'reflection-in-action' is enhanced by actual practice that will trigger the development of 'best principles'. As we claimed before, learning cannot be abstracted from actual practice. Concepts that are detached from practice distort or obscure elements that practice. Without a clear understanding of these elements and the role they play it is impossible to fully understand neither certain phenomena nor their concepts.

This level is concerned with understanding the origin, nature and validity of knowledge and is also intended to help students develop an integrative insight into managerial phenomena as well as into the art of inquiry, (or what was previously called a theory of inquiry), by learning to ask pertinent questions.

This 'reflection-in-action' level is based on several elements. Firstly, tools, activities, and the pedagogical metaphors that we proposed all play a crucial role. Business simulations, personal journals, action-learning, in-company projects, multidisciplinary case studies, experiential exercises, and testimonials by executives: these are only some of the tools that can be used.

Driven as it is by its pedagogical philosophy, the 'travelling' and 'growing' metaphors, one of the Hybrid Business School pillars is the very practical management experience that can only be acquired by 'doing'. Action-learning projects provide an ideal opportunity to 'practise' management. The assumption is that students can learn more effectively with and from managers and teachers while all are engaged in the solution of actual, real-time and real-life problems occurring in a work-setting, applying the normal business pressures and constraints of organizational realities to ensure a high-quality outcome. Real-life, in-company projects not only provide the student with hands-on integrative experience, but also creates an immediate, and tangible contribution to and return on investment for the firm. Moreover, project work is a unique way of assessing whether the student is able to apply the knowledge he has acquired within the specific context of a particular company. For the student, the project provides an opportunity to integrate knowledge, skills and attitudes within one exercise, while teachers provide enabling constraints and take the role of experienced guides. The guide points out the way, provides navigation tools, and coaches personal development.

The 'travelling' and 'growing' metaphors obviously also contribute to the teaching philosophy. Teachers act as tutors, mentors, facilitators and helpers within a subtle mixture of coaching, negotiated authority and learned freedom. In this process, the teacher sometimes takes responsibility for learning, for example by pointing students to the knowledge base and learning material, experts and providers, or by directing group sessions or discussions within the learning community. Sometimes the responsibility for learning is shifted to students, for example by setting a particular pace or taking a particular approach according to the individual's learning style. Students work with their mentors and learn by observation and practice. Hence, it is a subtle mixture of education and knowledge creation. In this way, the individual learner can develop an epistemology of inquiry.

The tutor also needs to constantly assess the learner's progress. A combination of tutor assessment and self-evaluation by the student is one possible procedure and may result in a constructive learning process for the student.

A second important aspect is the learning laboratory and collaborative platform. As was demonstrated before, the integrated curriculum design that focuses on business, organizational, and managerial processes will work towards the use of such a learning laboratory. It provides people with opportunities to talk coherently about beliefs and attitudes, to comment upon them, question them, to look more clearly at sources and principles, to reflect upon them, to experiment with and finally apply them. The collaborative platform widens this perspective somewhat, making it more than just a group session. Program heads, faculty members, executives, advisory boards, corporate action-learning sponsors, and students together engage in developing new understandings, approaches and unlimited perspectives. This peer learning proves to be very efficient. Guided by the teacher, participants can experiment and apply newly acquired knowledge, behaviors and skills. Both platform and learning laboratories can be organized virtually or face-to-face. Members will also find the moral and emotional support for learning.

Thirdly, 'communities-of-practice', or the network of practitioners, are a last important item of this 'reflection-in-action' level. Offering an integrated view on working, learning and innovation within a particular corporate context and community in which the work actually takes place, 'communities-of-practice' are important areas for sustained individual learning to take place. As with learning laboratories, 'communities-of-practice' can be organized virtually or face-to-face. Alumni can play an important double role in such communities: both as a provider of experience, i.e., an expert, and as a learner themselves. because of its inherent flexibility, the Hybrid Business School acts as a facilitator in this dynamic life-long affiliation to such 'communities-of-practice'.

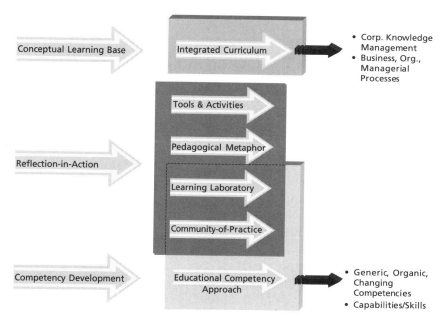

Figure 5.3 The Hybrid Business School's overall learning strategy

At the same time, these 'communities-of-practice' also cause organizational double-loop learning to take place as they aid the combination of mental models and changes in a community's 'way of seeing'. From a corporate point of view, the Hybrid Business School-based management education effort magnifies the firm's knowledge base as well as its knowledge network. Therefore, the Hybrid Business School should always take into account the corporate knowledge management effort. The Hybrid Business School is an important vehicle for a continuous learning process, and hence knowledge-creating innovation processes. This dynamic learning process is aimed at enhancing individual and corporate learning, and not just at transferring ideas or knowledge during one learning moment.

Competency Development

A last level is the development of competency as well as the overall educational competency framework. Generic, organic and changing competencies are about the ability to create new businesses and strategic resources, technologies and capabilities, and products and services. They put great emphasis on the capacity of individuals to constantly learn about their own performance, objectives and capabilities within ever-changing contexts, and in the light of this learning, to change, and to learn from the change. Competencies are also about the leap from information to knowledge by giving meaning to the flow information and involvement in organizational contexts. The Hybrid Business School concept can be of added value to corporations as it enables them to also focus on organic competencies. Unlike generic competencies, that refer to the more abstract competencies that can be applied across organizations and different roles, organic competencies describe organization-specific competencies that arise from a specific role (i.e., they are role-unique and context-specific). In other words, starting from their own customized competency model, firms can incorporate these organic competencies into a company-wide organizational development project that reflects and incorporates their core values and culture. Both the learning community and the 'community-of-practice' will play an important role in developing competencies and ensuring double-loop learning.

In addition, the educational competency approach focuses on the development of capabilities. Capabilities describe, for instance, the behavioral skills needed to communicate, to work as a member of a team, and to understand the dynamics of the context of manager's jobs. They help people to develop and sustain competencies by means of continuous learning, almost as a genetic sequence of evolutions. Finally, a personal development path completes the educational competency approach.

The Hybrid Business School's Delivery Dimension

Learning is considered to be a dynamic process of constant development, experience and growth. Learning provides individuals with the opportunity to pause, reflect upon and reframe both personal issues and experiences and those of others. Learning styles and pace will be important individual drivers. Indeed, learning is not abstract but contextual: it happens at the appropriate time, in the appropriate dose with the proper experience so that it can be immediately applied. As such, learning can be seen as the process whereby knowledge is created through the transformation of experience, 'know-how' and 'know-why'.

Pedagogical Material

The learner is the focal point in the learning process. Rather than creating a pre-set and fixed body of knowledge, which would define the profession of management, the learner searches for issues, looks for the appropriate information, comes up with questions, and thus discovers management. It is up to the learner to define what is 'appropriate'. Hence, the overall aim for the student is to focus on his or her personality. The student is pictured as a garden in which everything is already planted, but still needs to grow.

Earlier, we used the metaphor of a motorbike. On a motorbike, as Pirsig argues, the driver is part of nature. He feels and smells nature and is able to react much faster to changes in nature. This analogy suggests that learners have to be in touch with their environment – riding their bike – in order to develop a feel for events and their backgrounds. As we are talking about a dynamic movement, learners should constantly be paying attention to their surroundings and remain alert. When we have seen, we travel and grow, hence learn.

In other words, the learner develops and designs his own body of knowledge using his own learning style. Technology, such as hypertext platforms, facilitates this process. The hypertext platform, which we will explain later in more detail, not only offers that flexibility, but also accommodates a multitude of learners and myriads of learning paths. It produces new realities, new meaningful contexts, each with their own particular 'grammar', and thus creates a unique management rhetoric for the student.

The pedagogical material used by the Hybrid Business School, in short, is organized differently from its classical functional textbook format in order to accommodate the hypertext platform. Not only does the electronic form alter the delivery, it also reflects the overall learning strategy depicted earlier. Three categories can be distinguished:

1 Concept/principle library.
1 Case/illustration library.
2 Activity learning set.

Subject matters are seen as a set of experiences each student should absorb. The concept/principle library provides a common language for understanding, a learning base which reflects the minimum level of what a manager should 'know'. The library, however, will have to be developed in such a way that it fits the logic of the integrated curriculum.

The case/illustration library may include cases covering a broad range of ideas from different industries, company-specific issues, organizational processes, or a combination of these elements. Each case illustrates an in-depth description to capture the underlying elements of a certain strategy, decision, policy or process. This means the cases are more than just anecdotal as they offer a deeper conceptual understanding by showing how concepts were applied (know-how) as well as the underlying logic (know-why). Given the hypertext approach, these cases will only be used when relevant to the student and hence related to a specific challenge with which a student is faced at a particular moment. The link with the case-based reasoning system discussed in the previous chapter is clear. Such a system helps indexing each case so that learners can find 'similar cases', or it can generate details regarding a particular decision and explaining failures. If there is no case that exactly matches the given situation, then the system will select the most similar case. An adaptation procedure can be encoded in the form of adaptation rules. The result of the case adaptation is a solution, but it also generates a new case that is automatically added to the case library. Consequently, it can be used as a learning device, but also as an input for a knowledge base. This process of learning and knowledge-building helps develop 'best principles'. Working with principles teaches participants to develop a conceptual and cohesive mindset about management as well as a theory of practice; this will help them develop their strategic analysis skills.

This is further put into practice in our last category of activity learning. Within the hypertext platform, this category refers to tools, applications, and exercises in which the student will be actively involved. This will enable him to translate a managerial phenomenon to a conceptual level, come to an understanding by asking pertinent questions, and translate that understanding back to a practical level, i.e., to develop critical distance. Within a broader framework, there is a clear link to action-learning projects, 'communities-of-practice' and competency development. The development of competencies plays an important role as they enable students to turn information into knowledge.

The hypertext platform, of which the Internet is the perfect illustration, allows users to inter-link elements from these three categories, using their own individual strategy and learning path. These inter-linkages can be horizontal (i.e., within categories), vertical (between categories), or a combination of both. For example, when a student reads a text about one concept and encounters a reference to another, he or she can link this to information about the other concept by simply clicking the mouse. The same holds true for the case and illustration library. When a student reads about a concept, a link can be made to a case that illustrates the application of this concept. Similarly, a text about a company case can be linked to any concept that is mentioned or to some activity-learning exercises.

This allows a learner to focus on exactly what interests him, and thus enhances learning possibilities. It also allows students to understand managerial paradoxes, portraying a confusion or collapse of different logical levels as they do. It is, of course, the role of the tutor to organize material in such a way that it makes sense in terms of the particular target group. It would be unrealistic to think that any Hybrid Business School could ever produce material that perfectly contextualizes a company's and individual's environment.

On the other hand, the hypertext format enables fast, continuous development and adaptation of the case library (or any of the other libraries) without having to alter the other categories at the same time. What with the rapidly changing economic and business realities, the electronic platform is of special added value to companies and individual participants. In other words, it concerns a dynamic system in which the different categories each have their own dynamic pace. These dynamics are caused by the company's approach to knowledge management and organizational learning, its corporate strategy, philosophy and vision, the strategic use of management development initiatives, and the development of subject matters and management itself.

The Hybrid Business School environment can only be realized with considerable IT effort. IT, however, is a tool and not an end in itself. Consequently, we will be looking at using the appropriate technologies driven by strategic instinct, performance improvement, 'communities-of-practice', and especially human design. It is IT that accommodates the individual and not, as so often is the case, the other way around. This approach is what some people would call a Japanese approach to using information technology.

Figure 5.4 represents the Hybrid Business School's delivery dimension. As a pedagogical software environment, Lotus Learning Space or Microsoft's MLT can be used. Compared to the hypertext database, the Lotus Learning Space software has other advantages. Increasingly, these platforms produce new releases that offer greater flexibility and more scope for integration.

A typical learning environment should offer:

- Schedules (guidelines, monitoring).
- A media center or resources with hypertext links to:
  - managerial concepts;
  - case/illustrations;
  - managerial skills or competencies.
- A course room for discussions, debating, and the formation of a knowledge-web.
- Video-conferencing facilities.
- Participant profiles (in order to facilitate the formation of dynamic networks or communities).

146

- Assessment manager (with degree courses).
- Links to outside software (e.g., HRM software).

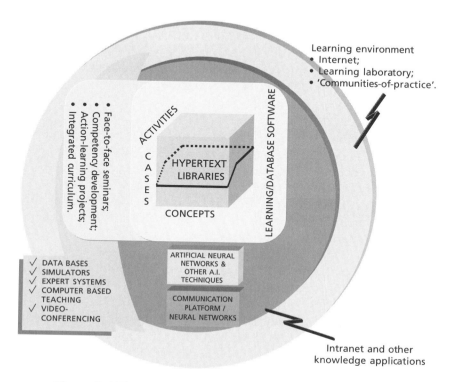

Figure 5.4 The Hybrid Business School's delivery dimension

People who share experiences create knowledge. When people enjoy their jobs, they identify with their jobs and put their all in it. They will be willing to learn and adapt since they are not feeling threatened by rules and regulations. They are free to come up with an idea or a proposal, and will pay attention to detail since they will observe matters they have not seen before and will enjoy it. Attention to detail is a basic attitude for quality improvement. In addition, quality is also the ability to really see to issues. By identifying with underlying signifiers, these signifiers will 'talk'. Managers should therefore be attentive and take their time in order to create a critical distance.

Pedagogical Concerns and Non-Virtual Delivery

Presenting pedagogical material in an electronic format is appropriate in terms of applying the 'travelling' and 'growing' metaphors, that form the basis of the Hybrid Business School's pedagogical philosophy. The general set-up of the concept is well-complemented by a system that allows tutors and students to easily access those concepts relevant. This is the main advantage of the electronic format over the text book format.

Typically, business schools use IT as an alternative to the classroom situation in order to reduce their overheads. It has, however, often been unsuccessful as a learning delivery mode since it still supports the traditional delivery paradigm, i.e., the transfer theory. Here, IT plays the role of intellectual forklift or crane filling the assumedly empty vessel. As argued earlier, the use of IT with the transfer metaphor only magnifies its weaknesses.

Any use of IT, particularly in terms of learning technologies, should be based on the conversational paradigm that is reflected by the 'travelling' and 'growing' metaphors. Here, knowledge here is shaped by the tools of inquiry and therefore by conversation, emphasizing the importance of tutorials. It is this focus on conversation that makes the Internet such a success. The Hybrid Business School hypertext approach is based on that Internet technology concept. Tutorials, projects, 'communities-of-practice', and face-to-face events should all contribute to reinforcing that conversational paradigm.

5-3 Summary

- A Hybrid Business School delivers flexibility in time and space but also in the discovery of the management field. Hence, it is oriented towards the manager who is looking for the appropriate knowledge and educational context.
- A Hybrid Business School approach is built on the acceptance that different types of knowledge contribute to the development of managers.

- A Hybrid Business School delivers individualized learning, based on previous knowledge and experience, present role and specific needs. It also allows for different forms of learning and different aspects of what should be learned.
- This necessitates a particular pedagogical approach which differs from the one-way broadcast delivery that is still prevalent. The Hybrid Business School's focal point is learning as opposed to teaching. Its pedagogical approach is learner-centered: the learner himself is mainly responsible for his own learning process (self-organized learning).
- A Hybrid Business School environment allows for non-linear dynamic learning and flexible learning alternatives.
- A Hybrid Business School offers integrated learning. Management is not the equation of different disciplines. Education should not be based on functions but on competency, supplemented by a project-based approach.
- The added value of a Hybrid Business School mostly consists of the interaction of the company's knowledge management approach as well with human resources management and management development strategies.
- A Hybrid Business School integrates virtual and non-virtual delivery. Learning cannot be solely virtual.
- A Hybrid Business School is the answer to both a company's need to create its own corporate university and the need for such a university to keep an outward look.
- In a Hybrid Business School, competencies are as important as a sound knowledge base.
- A Hybrid Business School relies heavily on the introduction of 'communities-of-practice': a network of practitioners.

Chapter 6

Building a Hybrid Business School: Guidelines for Implementation

If you have been watching the creation of the Hybrid Business School's building stones and concept, now is the time to think about developing that idea into an actual project to serve your company or program needs. It is clear why we have chosen the term 'hybrid'. The Hybrid Business School not only combines the corporation's knowledge management approach with individual development, business, management, and organizational processes, but it also merges a virtual (on-line) delivery with 'live' workshops. The need for the latter is clear from experiences with virtual delivery, but is also a direct consequence of the learning and the educational competency-based approach we have been advocating throughout this book. The content of workshops and the way to teach them (or rather, provide coaching) is very different from what happens today in most classroom situations. Within the appropriate learning-to-learn culture, the Hybrid Business School will cause an upward spiral of organizational learning.

Given the Hybrid Business School formula, we doubt whether it is a desirable or appropriate educational approach for undergraduate students, even though it is technically and organizationally possible, and they certainly have the right attitude for IT-based teaching. For reasons listed earlier, we have concentrated on graduate and post-graduate education for both our research and this book, with a strong focus on the in-company courses.

It is clear that one does not need to adopt the complete Hybrid Business School platform in order for a particular learning project to be successful. It depends on what is being organized: a degree program open to all, a company-specific degree program, or a corporate management development initiative that is part of a broader training scheme or HRD strategy. For companies aiming to move rapidly into the knowledge era, however, the infrastructure described in the previous chapter may prove to be an important basic condition – a necessary basic condition, but one that still needs further development.

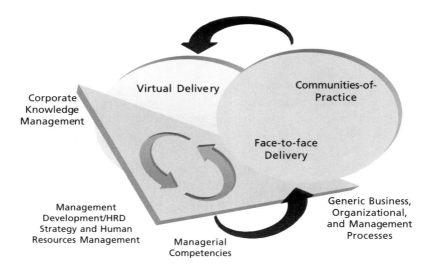

Figure 6.1 The Hybrid Business School dimensions

In the next paragraphs a corporate learning project will be described; also a degree program will be illustrated. It is clear that our concept has not been built by hitting just one home run. It has been constructed with a particular philosophy in mind, consistently hitting singles, doubles, triples, and home runs before, during, and after the start of the game. To guide you in the construction of your own Hybrid Business School, we would like to share a blueprint that contains a number of key issues for a successful implementation which can be applied to any given situation.

6-1 A Corporate Hybrid Learning Project

One example can be drawn from a European-American telecommunication network services firm, offering pan-European and transborder customized network solutions for voice, data, video, graphics service levels, and bandwidths. Initially, the firm experienced a

very steep and fast growth curve. Consequently, the number of employees increased rapidly. Most staff were highly skilled and edu-
cated expatriates. Then, because of the nature of its technology, the
complexity of solutions offered, and the fact that the firm was trying to create a complete new business, required a high learning
curve for the organization and its employees. Hence, a HRD strategy
was required that would serve individual development opportunities as well as the company's growth processes.

In the early stages, senior management already understood that the
company not only needed a well-defined knowledge management
approach, but also that its organizational development would have
to be built on strategic resources and technologies, and capabilities
that were flexible enough to change over time. They felt it would be
important to build a company culture and philosophy based on a
small set of values in order to offer continuity within the turbulence
of continuous change. The HRD strategy would have to support and
transcend these challenges.

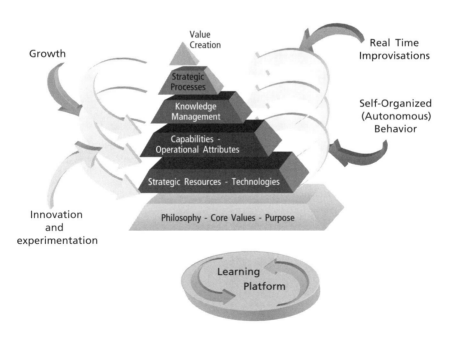

Figure 6.2 Challenges for a corporation's learning project

Let us make some of these elements more tangible. First of all, a small set of general guiding values and principles – the first part of the core philosophy – was defined during a number of workshops with senior and middle management. As is advocated by Collins and Porras, these values were considered to be the organization's essential and enduring beliefs, not to be compromised for financial gain or short-term expediency. Next, the second part of the firm's philosophy, the core purpose was defined, which is the organization's fundamental reason for existence, like a guiding star on the horizon. The outcome of the exercise for this company is shown below.

Values:
- Lead the European network services revolution.
- Amaze our customers with our reliability, quality, and high level of service in customizing networking solutions.
- Empower creative individuals.

Purpose:
- 'Complexities made simple'.

The impact of this philosophy on the organization was enormous. For example, contracts with staff, suppliers, and clients became more transparent. The firm became more careful in dealing with underlying technical issues for customers, partners, and shareholders. Further, the philosophy determines the definition of operating practices, business processes and the organizational structure. In short, the entire business and product concept is guided by and assessed according to the 'complexities made simple' purpose.

The firm's knowledge management approach was organized around focus groups. These focus groups consisted of people from different departments who were involved in a similar issue, for example, one relating to business development or customer support. Let us go into the last example. The customer support center had a help desk that was accessible 24 hours a day, seven days a week, and was the single point of contact for customers seeking technical information or the answer to a problem. It was also responsible for informing customers about maintenance and upgrading activities. Using an

IT-based support system that was shared by the customer support center, the network operations center, and representatives in key footholds throughout Europe, direct feedback and technical information could be given to customers.

This focus group also had access to a knowledge management system that consisted of two main parts. First of all, the system was aimed at creating knowledge. Members of the focus group therefore developed (electronic) stories about customer challenges and issues to see how they were handled. Templates were available to simplify this work; these pinpointed the practices and principles behind them. These stories were then screened by peers and retained as new cases, or added to existing stories. The story-approach was chosen because stories enabled employees to understand complicated issues in an accessible way. Secondly, the system was geared towards sharing this knowledge. A search option was added to the system so that at all times, members of the focus group could access the knowledge data base in order to search for similar issues and for contacts who were involved in these earlier stories. The system worked like a central communication hub so that group members did not have to keep on 'reinventing the wheel', were able to offer the customer better service, as well as save time and increase internal efficiency.

Once this direction was taken, senior management created an environment to encourage employee knowledge-sharing. The Human Resources Department then started to develop processes and policies to encourage and reward employees to engage in a 'life-long' learning path and consistently share that knowledge with others. Senior management seriously backed this initiative. Also, the HR department developed a company-specific competency model, together with a tool enabling employees to zoom in on the competencies and knowledge they lacked or needed to improve upon. The competency model was also used as a tool to measure evaluations linked to compensation and benefits. New employees were screened for their desire to learn and transfer knowledge. The focus groups were made guardians of this new culture in order for the company to maintain 'out-of-the-box thinking' and to carry on 'exploring the boundaries of the unknown'.

The HRD department was then made a 'Eurobrand' business center, which was a high priority strategic leader and business partner with ample resources, looking for strategic alliances with European business schools. This clearly reflected the function of HRD: to create and deploy coherent programs on a Pan-European level, and to offer customized solutions for individuals and focus groups. HRD 'owns' the European HRD processes and initiates programs and courses, establishes standards, identifies providers, monitors quality, provides information, internal marketing, and manages logistics and enrollment. In this process, the focus groups and senior management are seen as contributors and influencers as well as coaches to employees and first-line managers. Within the Hybrid Business School concept, they will also act as 'communities-of-practice'. The HRD department appointed an outside consultant to help develop a HRD strategy, coordinate the role-out of the corporate learning center, and, later on, to act as an intermediate between the company and different educational partners.

Corporate strategy and vision, the business future, the 'big picture', and employability is what an HRD strategy is based on. It consists of one competency model and three levels. Employees are able to participate in a number of topics on each level, and in this way follow a horizontal path. Alternatively, learners can choose for a vertical path by digging deeper in certain related subjects. In other words, the three levels blend into each other.

The initial level deals with relatively basic topics. Next is the managerial competency line annex personal learning plan. For this example, we clearly show some generic and organic competencies as well as some capabilities that were specified within the corporate model. Existing as they do across the organization in varying degrees of importance and mastery, generic competencies refer to more abstract competencies, to an epistemology of inquiry reflecting thought processes, a theory of practice, a deeper understanding of reflective practices, and critical distance. The ability to articulate a (shared) strategic vision, communicate and translate that vision throughout the organization, and enable organizational members to realize that vision is part of generic competence. The ability to encourage double-loop learning involving the ability to translate a managerial phenomenon into a conceptual level, come to an un-derstanding, and translate that understanding back to a practical level, is another.

'Changing competencies' and competencies of changeability in-clude emerging, transitional, and maturing competencies, which refer to those competencies that will be increasingly relevant over the years (emerging), the competencies that are becoming less rele-vant (maturing), or competencies that may become less relevant while their emphasis increases (transitional). For this particular company, competencies were included that related to network and telecommunications technologies and competencies related to the changing customer demands as well as the changing business struc-ture. A number of capabilities were also covered by the competency-track. Capabilities such as personal effectiveness, negotiation skills, time management, team skills, cross-cultural awareness, and com-munication skills were considered fundamental.

Again, a horizontal as well as vertical path can be distinguished. Also, it is clear that the different competencies are intertwined at the level of the content driven topics. The company thought com-petencies had to reflect the leap from information to knowledge which gives meaning to the flow of information within organiza-tional contexts.

The final level deals with strategic issues connected with future business and organizational processes. Topics on this level can be linked, and learners can also gain a deeper insight into topics by moving from one level to another. Of course, the hypertext enables and allows learners to 'play' with the different levels by jumping from one to the next; the same goes for concepts, cases, and activi-ties.

For each level, a number of modules have been defined. Each theme or module is characterized by three red lines, representing the 'big picture', an organizational theme and a personal theme. All con-cepts, cases, and activities will be presented within the context of these three themes.

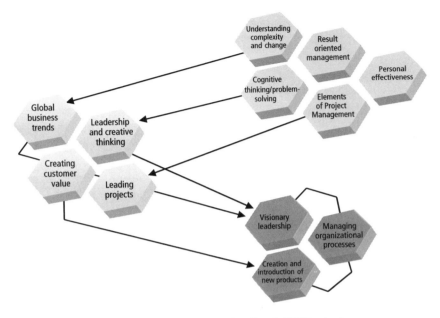

Figure 6.3 Highlights of the firm's HRD strategy

The figure above exemplifies one such module; at the same time, it depicts a possible path of development for the employees to follow.

Next, a ' Hybrid Learning Center' was set up. Catchy Lotus Notes pages were used for internal marketing and to provide information about learning objectives, course contents, didactic approach, background of the tutors, prerequisites, and so on. Again, all of this fits in with the auto-educational aspect. It is the learner who designs his own body of knowledge using his own learning style.

Also, electronic versions were made of the competency-assessment tool and personal learning plan. Once an individual's competency model was made, the employee in question discussed it with a coach who then guided him or her towards a particular learning track. As employees advance in the organization, their competency needs change, and so do their personal learning plan. This fact directly proves the need for a learning mindset in the organization, meaning that auto-education should be a strategic process that pervades organizational processes. The process also helps the employee understand his or her strengths and weaknesses and the direction he or she may want to take within the organization. Focus group managers play a role in this guidance process, too. In addition to their guidance input, they will consider which action-learning projects could provide the employee with an ideal opportunity to practise management. Finally, apart from the on-going assessment during the individual learning sessions, there is also self-evaluation and tutor assessment.

The company next set up an electronic enrollment, and follow-up system. It identified, acquired, or developed business simulations, personal journals, action-learning in-company projects, multi-disciplinary case studies and illustrations, experiential exercises, and an activity learning set (tools and applications). For each topic, subject matters were identified with which to construct a concept or principal library. The cases and illustrations used covered a broad range of ideas and in-depth descriptions of the 'know-how' and 'know-why' of different industries, economic trends, company-specific issues, organizational processes, or any combination thereof.

For each module, program heads, faculty members, senior managers, in-company action-learning project sponsors, and students were brought together, both virtually and face-to-face, in a learning laboratory. This laboratory enabled people to discuss their assumptions in 'real time' – at the very moment they are dealing with an issue. This practice area enabled people to talk coherently about beliefs and attitudes, to comment upon them, question them, to look more clearly at sources and opportunities. In addition, the focus group to which the participant belongs, acts as a 'community-of-practice'. This 'community-of-practice' is important for the development of competencies, as it combines the 'know-how' and 'know-why' with on-the-job possibilities for practice, and also ensures double-loop learning takes place. It was clear that the key to success was support for and active involvement of every member of the focus groups. As a result, what the company did next was to devise a number of learning exercises for the various focus groups in support of the learning culture, thus showing the advantage for all involved.

6-2 Building a Corporate Learning Project according to the Hybrid Business School Concept

Thus far, we have given examples of methodological and content-related issues for a Hybrid Business School approach in a corporate context.

In practice, a student or employee joins the learning project via an in-company project. In other words, the employee undertakes a project dealing with a current company issue, such as introducing a product on a new market, innovation processes, an IT network for distributed learning, etcetera. This project will form the backbone of the developing learning process as the student incorporates the concepts, applications and skills. Based on the project, a personal learning trajectory can be identified, which includes study of concepts (out of the subject matter database), case studies, activities, and some workshops. There is no difference in the process, whether or not the company aims at organizing a learning project that should result in a degree. In case a degree is desirable, the company is obliged to cooperate with a Business School that can deliver such a degree. At the same time, the in-company project can grow into a degree thesis, if required.

Before going into detail with a 'to do' list, we must highlight some important boundary conditions. One of the most important key success factors is the constant and active support of senior management, as it is responsible for shaping the organization's learning culture and knowledge management approach. If senior management is unable to build a learning environment that allows and supports constant (on-line) learning, then the Hybrid Business School approach will only have limited success. This learning environment is a necessary and important link between corporate strategy and the changing role of management as depicted in chapter 1. Senior management plays a key role in acting as a catalyst for creating the learning environment. It must play an advisory role and allow personnel to take part in management development activities. The learning environment must be supported by a clearly defined internal and external communication strategy. It is important to constantly communicate the links between strategy, HR development, training, knowledge management, and the learning platform. If a company is unable to do this itself, external help should be contracted. Given the financial investment in this learning approach, internal branding is an important issue.

A second prerequisite is that line management should also be supportive of the learning approach. It must create a culture of learning, that can be translated into the daily practice of each employee. Of course, job evaluations should have a focus on developmental issues, and it should be made easy for the learner to apply what he or she learns. The learner also should be enabled to make the transition between what is learned and the daily practice.

These boundary conditions might not sound new, as it is generally understood that the support of senior management is crucial to the learning process. In our experience, however, there have been too many cases in which support existed on paper, and not in practice. In too many cases, management does not regard development to be a valued management practice that it should actively guide and support. There are numerous cases in which line management was not given the tools to support their staff in their development endeavor, where senior management lost interest after a couple of months ('it is good for internal and external PR if we do this'), and colleagues were not enabled to transfer learning.

Finally, appointing an independent program coordinator is crucial to the development of a successful learning project. If need be, this could be an external (interim) manager. This coordinator needs to possess knowledge on and experience with the pedagogical and methodological approach because he or she will liaise between the participants (the learners), the educational providers (institutions and their staff/faculty/tutors), and the firm (HRD and HR responsibles, senior management). The coordinator must brief faculty about the company and its specific issues, the participants, the learning project, the contribution of individual faculty members for the learning project – also to create synergies -, corporate and individual development paths, and assess the overall quality of the professors and 'classes'.

The coordinator is often involved, from the onset, in the project's development and the identification of the educational partners and/or faculty. He or she will play an overall coaching role for the participants. Hence, the coordinator also needs to have the necessary academic credibility, combined with corporate credibility, and an expertise in organizational and strategic analysis as well as management processes.

Let us now turn to our 'to do' list that a company should follow in order to create a hybrid learning project.

1 First of all, define and implement a knowledge management approach and overall HRD strategy. In essence, the knowledge management approach, the corporate strategy and vision, organizational and managerial processes, and the HRD strategy will drive the themes for a corporate learning project. The company can gather its specific educational needs from this exercise. At the same time, a number of in-company student projects should be defined.

2 Integrate pedagogical material in a hypertext environment, focusing on the broader corporate theme(s) of the learning project. No one particular functional course should be identifiable in this hypertext database of pedagogical material. A broad integration of concepts and their interdependencies is more important than a thorough understanding of any particular concept. The more concepts, cases and activities are inter linked, the richer the database will be, and the more potential learning paths can be created. In light of the individualized learning agendas, the richness and complexity of this inter linking is of paramount importance. Also, the integrated database should provide enough breadth and depth to to be used stand-alone and to cater to all possible needs for learning about management on an advanced level. Both the functional and technical design of this hypertext environment require careful attention; the amount of work necessary for developing it should not be underestimated. In most cases, it is done in close cooperation with an educational partner.

3 Three kinds of information sources need to be added within the framework of the pedagogical database. The first extension is to

create a link to an electronic library, containing reference material and articles in an electronic, 'browsable' and 'searchable' format. The second extension should provide students with direct
access to general information sources or (company) databases,
e.g. to *the Financial Times* or *Gartner Information Services*. Finally, it
can be interesting to link some specific, but more detailed courses
(such as web-based courses, or CD-ROMs) that allow students to
explore further any particular area of interest.

4   Ideally, in-company speakers, together with staff from the educational partner, will develop their own pedagogical (subject matter
or concept/principle) database. The company should remember
to discuss copyright; also, non-disclosure issues should be re-
searched. If publicly available pedagogical material is used, copyright laws should be respected. The legal issues on copyright for
electronic material are still vague.

5   Faculty members play a crucial role in the Hybrid Business
School, as they have to radically change their pedagogical approach and their practical involvement. Faculty members, subject specialists, and guest speakers possibly need some kind of re-
training in order to become true mentors and guides rather than
teachers, and to come to a thorough understanding of the pedagogical concept of the Hybrid Business School. The project and
activity focus is another area where staff may need coaching.

6   Build a company case base around the themes of the learning
project. A case base needs to be understood as a set of pedagogical
cases or lived experiences. Cases are examples of applications of
concepts in a particular industrial, market, or company context.
The role of cases in the pedagogical database is a key connection
between knowledge management and virtual learning. The complexity of writing a process and hypertext based (multimedia)
case with clear links to the subject matter database should not be
underestimated. The least attractive possibility is using existing
teaching cases or other publicly available materials. This approach does not really fit in with the Hybrid Business School concept.

7 Students and staff should be able to communicate constantly via a communication technology network within an electronic learning environment. The choice of electronic learning environment is therefore important, as the wrong choice could constrain potential development. 'Communities-of-practice' should also be created in order to stimulate the learning process. Other key employees, experts, stakeholders, and academics can take part in these 'communities-of-practice'. They can learn from the students and their projects, and they can contribute their own experiences as well, offering them a flexible learning base for continuous self-education at minimum cost and effort.

8 A specific and detailed curriculum must be designed. This curriculum should be an optimal balance between the freedom and flexibility of learning according to the Hybrid Business School concept. The ultimate result will not necessarily be reached in the first attempt.

9 The personal development monitor should be used as a follow up on course delivery and the learning on the level of each individual employee. While the ideal would be to plug in the learning process with the personal development trajectory of the participants, other forms of evaluation could also be used. In some cases (for instance learning projects leading to a company MBA or other accredited degree), it could be advisable to go through a student selection process at the start of the program, by means of an entry test, an interview, or both. The entry test should focus on the student's learning attitude and related process variables, rather than simply on standard intellectual performance. It remains, however, a difficult task for a firm to decide on its criteria for selection.

10 The Hybrid Business School concept must be communicated clearly to potential students as it is important that their expectations match its philosophy.

6-3 An Example of a Degree Program based on the Hybrid Business School Concept

Next, a real-life case study will be discussed, which outlines the development of a degree program at the Euro-Arab Management School (EAMS) in Granada, Spain. EAMS is a project of the European Union supported by the Spanish Government and the Arab League. Emerging from the Euro-Arab dialogue as it did as a way to further develop economic relations between Europe and the Arab World, EAMS is mentioned in the Action Program of the 1995 Barcelona declaration for its contribution to the development of human resources, especially in the fields of professional training and educational technologies.

The EAMS mission is to prepare, through education, training and research activities, competent managers from both the Arab World and Europe. Its aim is to develop and promote, through a collaborative network of partner institutions in the Arab World and Europe, a better understanding of socio-economic and managerial issues that are central to the success of Euro-Arab relations. Most management development programs on either continent do not sufficiently address the cultural dimension underlying management concepts and practices. Furthermore, in today's global economy, it is increasingly important for managers to recognize differences in attitudes, values and traditions in their business dealings with others. It is therefore timely and of paramount importance to focus on cross-cultural management and surface-associated issues for study. In addition to disseminating that information to policy-makers and managers through conferences, seminars, workshops and publications, EAMS offers a number of programs.

A Master in the Management Development Program (MMDP) trains tutors from EAMS partner institutions, providing skills in bi-cultural (Euro-Arab) management and exposure to new pedagogical developments. The program targets faculty members and trainers who hold a degree in management or related fields. These tutors help deliver, within the framework of the Hybrid Business School, a degree program in their home countries which is called the Euro-Arab Management Diploma (EAMD). The method used in this large-scale EAMD is an interesting example of a Hybrid Business School.

The Euro-Arab Management Diploma (EAMD)

The EAMD is offered by the different partner institutions in their respective countries, in collaboration with EAMS, and using the EAMS pedagogical material. It targets managers involved or interested in Euro-Arab trade, working for firms ranging from family-run to multinationals. The EAMD is a ten-month program.

Since the desired outcome for the manager is to acquire a holistic view of managerial practice, a skills-driven approach is the best way to teach/tutor management at the post-experience level. At the same time, the educational project should fit in with each student's personal development path and individual expectations. In practice, it will be more difficult for a Business School to achieve this than for a company, and it will be an important change in the pedagogical approach of most Business Schools today. This approach implies a kind of a (moral) learning contract between the student and the Business School stipulating mutual expectations.

Learning Strategy

A hybrid learning program should focus on organizational or business processes, or be based on a particular in-company project that will form the backbone of the learning process. In this way, students will learn to deal with, for example, the introduction of a product on a new market, a possible merger, the implementation of an IT network architecture, etcetera. Based on this, a personal learning path can be identified, which will include studying concepts (out of the pedagogical database), case studies, activities, and workshops. The implementation of a Hybrid Business School program must take into account issues such as accreditation and recognition by the local or international market. Some more work will be necessary in order to identify the exact elements of accreditation.

Mass-individualization, in the context of a degree program, can best be realized through a personal learning contract between the learner and the school. An efficient medium of a personal learning contract is an in-company project. The learner enters the course on the condition that learning will be based on a project that he or she engages in throughout the duration of the course. During this 'learning by doing', faculty staff (facilitator, tutor) will guide the learner through the database of material. Those parts of the pedagogical database that are the best input for the project will be studied at the very moment that the learner needs the information.

At the same time, the project provides the tutor with an ideal opportunity to apply and adapt concepts to local economic and cultural conditions. The project, which is carried out in a particular company in a specific country, is an exercise relating to local circumstances. The locally adapted of the tutor is crucial. The added value of the tutor-based approach, as compared to the open learning approach, is most apparent in the tutor's role of guiding students through their project work.

Whereas the conventional management curriculum is determined mainly by fixed academic concerns, the EAMD curriculum is evolutionary in nature and adapted both to business and academic prerequisites. Hence, the EAMD tries to integrate academic excellence and business relevance.

As a result, the EAMD is designed as a self-tuition, tutor-based management development program. Tutorials are organized and conducted by local tutors (from the partner institution) who have been trained in Granada on the EAMS 'train-the-trainers program' which is called the Master in Management Development Program (MMDP). In addition to tutoring, the EAMD emphasizes the use of actual case studies and project-based or hands-on learning. Often, the project-based learning consists of working on a real project in the student's company; hence, it makes a direct business contribution and creates an immediate financial return.

Study Load

The overall workload of the student for the entire course must be comparable to that of a similar degree elsewhere. The mixture of theory, application and 'learning-by-doing' should be monitored to ensure they fit the degree requirements. The pedagogical aim of the course, however, should be to provide the best possible learning track, enabling the student to complete his project and to acquire the necessary knowledge and skills to manage future projects in complex environments.

The EAMD study load consists of course-related work (some self-tuition and some tutorials) and a project. The course work (to be done in a self-tuition, tutor-based mode) is based on bi-cultural, Euro-Arab course material produced by EAMS. It requires approximately 450 hours of self-tuition. It is complemented by tutoring sessions of, for instance, three hours once a week over a ten-month period, totalling roughly 150 hours. In all, the course work required for the EAMD will come to 600 hours.

Project work will consist of developing 'real-life' case study dealing with a particular business situation. The workload for the project/case study will come to 250 hours. This includes the different stages of the project up to the completion of the final report. The final report will be written for the company and a presentation will be made.

The total workload for the EAMD will amount to approximately 850 hours.

Admission, Assessment Criteria and Procedures

Each applicant needs to fill out an application form (with enclosures), to be obtained from the EAMS partner institution in his or her country. Upon return of the completed application, the partner institution will evaluate the candidate's credentials and decides whether or not to invite the candidate to take the Euro-Arab Management Diploma Admission Test (EAMDAT). This test is administered in different countries of the partner institutions, but processed by EAMS in Granada.

To be admitted to the EAMD program, a candidate must comply with the following criteria:
1 Be a university graduate.
2 Have had a minimum of two years' work experience.
3 Be proficient in English.
4 Pass the EAMD Admission Test (EAMDAT), which is comparable

to the GMAT test, but with less cultural bias.

Candidates who are not graduates may, in exceptional cases, be accepted into the EAMD program. The final admission decision is made by EAMS, based on the candidate's score in the EAMDAT test and on his or her application file.

Final assessment of the student's performance and the awarding of the EAMD is coordinated and administered by EAMS.

Program Design and Content Dimension

An example of a possible 'learning route' is given in figure 6.4, navigating the student through the pedagogical database. Let us assume that the subject of this route is organizational culture as the student's given starting point. From there, individual students can choose their own way. All possible connections (the before-mentioned concepts, cases and activities) can be reached by means of a simple hypertext link. From there, each student decides what other (related) concepts, cases and activities are of particular interest. The student designs his own learning path according to his own needs, knowledge base and learning style.

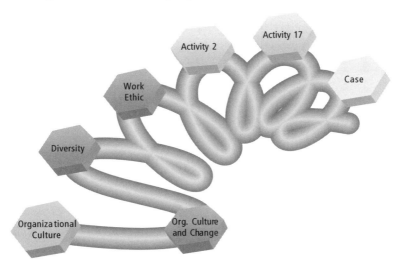

Figure 6.4 Example of a possible learning path

Figure 6.4 is merely a suggestion. In case of continuous learning (corporate education), the student can be much more flexible as to what, and in what order, he learns. The degrees of freedom for the student increase.

The student may, for example, start reading the definition of organizational culture. In this text, a number of hypertext links exist. He or she then decides to learn more about organizational culture and change. In this, again a number of hypertext links exist, each time referring to concepts, cases and activities. The student then decides to learn more about diversity. By clicking on the link, the student will be directed to that concept. From there, the student may choose to explore the concept 'work ethic'. In order to illustrate this concept, he or she may choose to try and apply the concept to a particular activity or exercise and therefore to click on, for instance, activity no. 2. Activity 2 turns out to be a short example of how companies manage diverse work ethics, and asks the student to write a short memo on how this concept is dealt with in his or her company. The student may then consult activity 17, which consists of a brief example on employment policies, taken out of a newspaper report, which the student can again relate to his or her own situation. The student may have become interested in the concept of corporate culture while doing activity 17. He or she may then go on to a suggested case on how three companies have implemented and managed organizational culture.

Delivery Dimension

Because the EAMD has been based on the 'travelling' and 'growing' metaphors of education and learning, many EAMS business school partners will need to shift from the subject-centered paradigm to the learner-centered paradigm. This learning philosophy is characterized in a number of different ways. The EAMD attempts to widen rather than deepen knowledge. The program provides as much flexibility as possible in terms of time and content. Attention is particularly given to developing managerial skills during sit-in sessions such as tutorials. The EAMD is project-based, not only for the above-mentioned reasons, but also in order to co-create new pedagogical material and new case material. Self-tuition is an integral part of the EAMD program, especially important given the need for flexibility and the time constraints of practicing managers. The concept behind the EAMD is not to train a chosen few, but rather to organize training programs so as to be able to reach as many people as possible. The local (corporate) cultural component should be contained within the EAMD. The tutor will play a crucial role in adapting any pedagogical material to local conditions. No approach will ever be able to produce pedagogical material that can accommodate all companies or even all departments in these companies. Hence, local adaptation must take place during the tutorials.

The process of material development involves de-constructing pedagogical material from its classical textbook format and isolating three categories:

1 Concept/ principle library (contextualized definitions with applications);
2 Case/illustration library (case studies and more extensive examples/ stories);
3 Activity learning set (with or without brief examples).

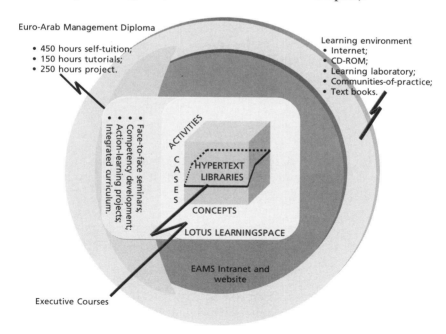

Figure 6.5 The concept of a Hybrid Business School applied to EAMS

Figure 6.5 represents EAMS and its EAMD. Although initially, the diploma was thought of as its 'raison d'être', now, EAMS's ultimate aim is to give any course relevant to the management of a particular company in any country. There is a growing demand from companies not so much for degree courses, but rather for short, specialized courses such as finance for engineers, or telecom in the Maghreb countries. With the pedagogical material presented in the form of an electronic database, partners can download the material they specifically need for a particular course. Once the hypertext database is complete, it will be very easy to access pedagogical material in order to create specialized degree courses.

EAMS has chosen Lotus Learning Space as the IT environment to support its pedagogical material. In addition to the hypertext database, the Lotus Learning Space software offers other advantages which will increasingly become important as the relevant technology will be developed and made widely accessible.

The Lotus Learning Space software offers the following:

- a schedule (guidelines, monitoring);
- a media center or resources with hypertext links to:
  - managerial concepts (independent of functional areas);
  - case studies and applications;
  - managerial skills or competencies;
  - a 'course room' for discussions;
  - profiles (of participants in order to facilitate the formation of networks or communities).

The pedagogical material is developed in an electronic format. If a paper-based format is preferred or needed, it can be produced on using the electronic format.

For tutors a more flexible format will mean greater choice of course materials. Tutors will be able to tailor programs to each individual's needs.

Tutors will play an important role in adapting any pedagogical material to the local circumstances if needed. It is unrealistic to think that EAMS can produce country-specific material for all of its clients. Thus, it should be possible to use pedagogical material as a 'general denominator'. In particular circumstances, however, some cases or even concepts would not apply, or some concepts may have to be applied differently. It is not the role of the tutor to write specific pedagogical material but rather to organize tutorials for each target group.

6-4 Building a Degree Program according to the Hybrid Business School Concept

At this stage it will be useful to try and summarize the procedure to create a degree program based on the Hybrid Business School concept. The 'to do' list we present here should not be seen as a fully-fledged plan of attack, as too much in this project depends on the target group and the management institute's pedagogical philosophy. The steps mentioned in this list, however, should be addressed for the implementation of a Hybrid Business School approach. Some of them may appear to be similar to the approach of regular Business Schools, but the issues to be solved differ substantially.

1 Identify and define the degree in terms of title, workload, essential components, etcetera, and the target group of this degree course. The choice for the Hybrid Business School concept requires a different pedagogical approach, which will have consequences for content and methodology. The expectations of the student should be managed in respect to the chosen methodology.

2 Build pedagogical material (integrated into each functional area) into a hypertext environment, using the subdivision of concepts, cases and activities. No one particular functional course should be identifiable in this hypertext database of pedagogical material. A broad integration of concepts and their interdependencies is more important than thorough understanding of any single concept. The more concepts, cases and activities are inter linked, the richer the database becomes and the more possible learning paths can be created. In light of the individualized learning agendas, the richness and complexity of this inter linking is of paramount importance. The integrated database should also provide enough

breadth and depth for stand-alone use and to cater to all possible needs for learning about advanced management. Both the functional and technical design of this hypertext environment must be carefully done, and the amount of work needed to develop should not be underestimated.

3   Although the integrated database is at the heart of the pedagogical approach, it is important to link it to further information. In practice, this means that three kinds of information sources need to be added within the framework of the pedagogical database (see figure 6.4). The first extension would be to build in access to an electronic library, containing books and articles in an electronic, 'browsable' and 'searchable' format. The second extension should provide students with direct access to general information sources or databases such as *the Financial Times* or *Gartner Information Services*. Finally, it may be of interest to link certain specific, more detailed functional courses (such as web-based courses, or CD-ROMs) that allow students to explore particular area of interest. Another advantage of this last extension is that it will be useful in the accreditation process in any particular legal framework or country, as in the classical educational and accreditation system, functional courses act as a parameter for recognition. Therefore, the value of the degree and the potential for accreditation will increase if more classical university accreditation systems are used (e.g., the AACSB accreditation in the U.S., or the EQUIS/EQUAL accreditation in Europe).

4   Ideally, faculty members will develop their own pedagogical database. If it is decided to use existing pedagogical material it is important to respect copyright laws. Although pedagogical material is available via intranet access throughout the world (albeit protected by passwords), electronic copyright laws are still unclear. In education, we are accustomed to working with books, for which the copyright laws are clear. The legal issues concerning copyright on electronic material and copyright on paper-based material used in an electronic environment are still vague. Publishers do not always have a clear-cut policy and are generally reluctant in allowing electronic use of their pedagogical material. The more progressive publishers experiment with electronic pub-

lishing and hopefully this will cause progress in this area. At the moment it still remains an important concern for the design and implementation of the Hybrid Business School concept.

5 Faculty members play a crucial role in the Hybrid Business School, as they have to radically alter their pedagogical approach and their practical involvement. Faculty staff need thorough explanation and possibly re-training to learn to become tutors, mentors and guides rather than teachers, and thoroughly understand the pedagogical concept of the Hybrid Business School. In the case of a mixed degree or corporate degree program, faculty members will need to link up with other (external or corporate) faculty or with subject specialists (such as managers of the partner companies). Another area where staff may need coaching is the project and activity focus.

6 Build a case base. Both the development of more general cases (e.g., based on projects of alumni and students) or the development of new (industry or company-specific) cases are very important. The complexity of writing a process and hypertext-based (multimedia) case with links to the subject matter database should not be underestimated. The least attractive possibility is using existing cases or other publicly available materials. This approach does not fit in with the Hybrid Business School concept.

7 Students and staff should be able to constantly communicate using a communication technology network within an electronic learning environment. Ergo, the choice of electronic learning environment is important, as it could constrain potential development. In most cases, staff and students should be equiped with a standard portable PC and software in order to avoid connection problems. 'Communities-of-practice' should also be created to stimulate the learning process. For business schools and management institutes, this will be an ideal opportunity to offer alumni life-long learning contracts. Alumni can take part in these 'communities-of-practice'. They can learn from the students and their projects, and they can contribute their own experiences, offering the students a flexible learning base for continuous self-tuition at minimum cost and effort.

8 A specific and detailed curriculum should now be designed. This curriculum should seek to balance the freedom and flexibility of learning according to the Hybrid Business School concept, and the requirements necessary for an accredited degree in any particular country. The ultimate result cannot always be expected to be reached at the first attempt.

9 It is necessary to go through a student selection process at the start of the program, using an entry test an interview, or both. The entry test should focus on the learning attitude and related process variables rather than on standard intellectual performance alone. It remains, however, a difficult task for business schools to decide on its criteria for selection. The learning process will consequently need to be constantly monitored with a view to qualification. The focus of measurement, however, with switch from 'content and result' to 'learning, improved process and attitude'.

10 The Hybrid Business School concept must be communicated clearly to potential students as it is important that their expectations match the philosophy.

The steps listed here should only be seen as a blueprint and will need to be adapted to specific situations and contexts. Culture will play an especially important role in the different international educational approaches. The blueprint, however, remains the same. The Hybrid Business School will look different depending on circumstances and country.

6-5 Wrapping It All Up

The American philosopher Rogers quite rightly stated that 'even if you are on the right track, you will be run over if you stand still'. This statement captures the essence of today's organizations. Given the new economic realities, the technological revolution, the collapse of time and space, non-linear change, and their impact on business, organizations, management, and managerial roles, firms need to be able to develop and reinvent themselves very quickly.

Learning and knowledge become increasingly important in this quest for renewal. The main themes are learning faster than the competition, and sharing knowledge rapidly within the company.

The question, however, is how to organize these knowledge and learning processes in such a way that both individual and organizational development are supported. This is what the Hybrid Business School concept does. The whole concept is summarized in the at once simple and complex triangle with which we started this chapter. The power of the triangle depends on the balance of all three points. The tension between them represents the intertwining of organizational and individual learning. As the company grows and renews, its markets expand and its business concept changes, therefore other triangles come into existence that can be linked to the first-generation triangle. It is this fly wheel that illustrates the continuous and dynamic nature of the Hybrid Business School concept.

In its intelligent use of new technologies, the Hybrid Business School is geared towards personal learning styles and the new roles today's managers play in organizations. The interaction between virtual delivery, face-to-face delivery, and 'communities-of-practice' offers an efficient and convenient platform for learning.

The main aim of the Hybrid Business School concept was to break with the traditional way of business education that has proven to be rather ineffective. As Albert Einstein said, 'if what you're doing today is what you did yesterday, then don't expect to see new results'. The 'transfer' and 'growing' metaphors make for a more inspired and appropriate kind of delivery. We feel the content must be based an integrated curriculum and a competency-driven approach. This combination will allow for learning to take place at the appropriate time, using the appropriate approach and quantity.

It is clear that the Hybrid Business School concept is still fluctuating, and is still in its infancy. As a tool, it needs to mature. Over the next few years, it will be our goal to monitor the Hybrid Business School market, gathering information on the experiences of companies that will start to work with this concept, in order to make it a true learning platform.

References

Collins, J. & Porras, J. (1996). *Building your Company's Vision. Harvard Business Review*, September-October, pp. 65-77.